Written by Debby Wallace and Daniel Coston
Photographs and editing by Daniel Coston
Interviews conducted by Debby Wallace and Daniel Coston
Designed by Adam Roth

Our thanks to all those whose stories and photographs are featured in the book, and to Adam Roth for his time and work on this book. Special thanks to Nick Karres, the Karres family, and everyone that worked at the Double Door Inn.

The opinions expressed in this manuscript are solely the opinions of the author and do not represent the opinions or thoughts of the publisher. The author has represented and warranted full ownership and/or legal right to publish all the materials in this book.

HOME OF THE BLUES:
A History of The Double Door Inn
All Rights Reserved. Copyright © 2017 Written by Daniel Coston, editing and photography by Daniel Coston V3.0

This book may not be reproduced, transmitted, or stored in whole or in part by any means, including graphic, electronic, or mechanical without the express written consent of the publisher except in the case of brief quotations embodied in critical articles and reviews.

Fort Canoga Press
fortcanogapress.com
FCP-007

PRINTED IN THE UNITED STATES OF AMERICA

HOME OF THE BLUES

A HISTORY OF
THE DOUBLE DOOR INN

Fort Canoga Press

THANKS

Our thanks to the following people, whose purchase of a special edition copy helped to fund the making of this book.

Keith Plyler
Shaun McDermott
Matthew Karres
Larry Lipscomb
Betsy Norton Stowe
Jeri Thompson
Jill & Mark Olson
Bob Nelson
Brian Dunn
Rita Miller
David & Kay Anderson
Richard Walt
Don Carras
Delta Moon
Janet & Don Profant
Michelle Mastenbrook
Rick Booth
Kelly Karres
Cole Karres
Larry Brundage
Phil Hensley
Michael Wallace
Molly & Dennis Coston
Dennis Kiel
Scott Benfield

This book is dedicated to the entire family of Nick and Matthew Karres, my children, Michael and Michelle, and my mentor, Janine K.
-Debby Wallace

For Sandra, George & Mary King, Nick Karres and everyone involved with the Double Door Inn story. Thank you for all the blood, sweat and beers.
-Daniel Coston

NIGHTHAWKS ONSTAGE, 1978.
Courtesy Double Door Inn archives

HOME OF THE BLUES

A HISTORY OF THE DOUBLE DOOR INN

Written by
Debby Wallace
and
Daniel Coston

THE DOUBLE DOOR INN, JANUARY 2, 2017.
Photo by Daniel Coston

INTRODUCTION

On January 2nd of 2017, the Double Door Inn held their final show. After 43 years, the longtime hub of the Charlotte, NC music scene had gone from being the dream of two brothers, to being recognized as one of the oldest blues music venues in the United States. Over that time, the list of those that passed through it grew to an astounding list of musicians. The greatest names of blues music, rock & roll, folk, zydeco, reggae, country, R&B and more. Endless nights of great music. The night that Eric Clapton jumped on-stage to play with members of Muddy Waters' band. The nights that Stevie Ray Vaughan, Avett Brothers, Drive-By Truckers and many others played there, on their way to greater fame. All of those nights, centered around a tiny stage in what had originally been the porch area of the former home. But after this night, the music and memories would come to a close.

People showed up at the Double Door Inn throughout the day. Some looking for a ticket for a show that had sold out weeks before. Others came to say hello, and say goodbye. News crews camped out in the parking lot, doing live reports on the venue's last hurrah. In the middle of all this, the Double Door's staff continued preparations. Answering phone calls, occasionally ignoring calls, and preparing their second home for its final, sold-out show.

Owner Nick Karres had been thinking about this night when he announced in March of 2016 that the venue would be closing. Central Piedmont Community College, which had recently begun to surround the Double Door, would be purchasing the land after having acquired the adjoining property. The decision had been tough to make, but he knew that if he didn't wait, he would have no choice. "It was obvious," says the club's founder, and longtime owner, Nick Karres. "There's no other conceivable way that they weren't going to buy in, and not claim eminent domain. Even when I opened, you knew that someday, the school was going to take that land over. Everything you see at the school now, was not there when we opened. If David Kavah, the land owner next to me, hadn't held out as long as he did, we would have been gone a long time ago."

Karres and his team, many of whom had been working with the venue for twenty to forty years, crammed a lot of celebrations into the Double Door's final weeks. "We packed a year's worth of shows into the last three months," Nick would later say. "It was crazy."

The venue's last nights were especially emotional. The Spongetones, one of the city's most enduring bands, played their final New Year's Eve show after playing at the Double Door for 37 years. On New Year's Day, the Charlotte Blues Society held their final blues jam. For one more night, the venue that had long billed itself as "Charlotte's Home Of The Blues" celebrated the music with their last Open Mic Jam. And at last, another of the Double Door's long-running traditions, The Monday Night Allstars, would be the ones to bring down the curtain. And would do so by bringing down the house, one more time.

As the doors opened at 7:30pm, patrons filed in quickly. It had been drizzling for much of the evening, as it had done the evening before. As people walked in, they took long looks around the venue. They said hello to doorman Todd Smith, who had worked the front door since 1985. They took photos of everyone, and everything that surrounded them. The Double Door had never been accused of being spotless. Over the years, it had sometime been referred to as The Dirty Floor by some. But on this night, all of the Double Door's well-worm character was a beautiful sight to all. It was very familiar to those that were there on this night, and something that many were struggling to let go of.

As the All-Stars took the stage at 9pm, they reminded the crowd that the night was a celebration. A last toast to the Double Door, the music and the people that had made the venue so special. The band would play three sets on this night, one more than they had at previous shows. As they kicked into their first song, the crowd began to sing and dance. Before they had to let go of the venue, they would all let go, all in the name of a celebration that was nearly a half-century in the making.

When the Double Door Inn first opened, brothers Nick and Matthew Karres had not intended to run a music venue. But the music and the people found them. The story of the Double Door Inn is the story of many, but within that is the story of one man, his family, and those that became his extended family. All in a place that had built as a small family home during the 1920s. A home that had once been owned by two of the most prominent families in Charlotte, and had been a popular lamp shop, even before the Double Door Inn first opened its doors in the final days of 1973.

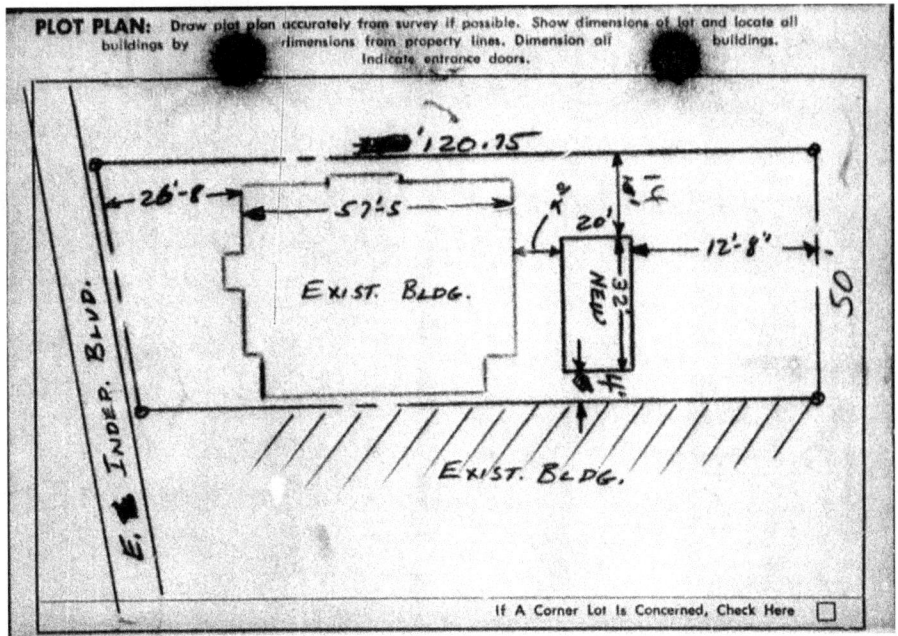

DESIGNS FOR PEGGY HOUSTON LAMP SHOP EXPANSION, INCLUDING
THE BUILDING OF THE DOUBLE DOOR'S FUTURE GAME ROOM.
Courtesy of the Main Library Of Charlotte

PEGGY HOUSTON LAMP SHOP
PRINT AD, 1966
Courtesy of Maria David/Retro CLT

CHAPTER ONE
218 Independence Boulevard
1973-1979

Nick Karres once shared a quote that in it's simplicity, says everything. After talking with him about keeping the Double Door going for so many years, one had to ask. Why would anyone spend their entire working life in a business that few enjoy, and even fewer can sustain for any length of time. He looked thoughtful for a moment and then said, "You either get it or you don't."

It has often been said that when you hear the blues, you know it. Through ups and downs, having commercial success or not, the music has endured. In that way, the Double Door Inn is quite similar to the blues music that it supported for so many years. The most important thing about blues music is that it evokes emotions with often simple stories as well as a distinctive beat. Some would argue that blues music began with W. C. Handy and his early compositions. Others believe that it began at the crossroads in the Delta when Robert Johnson, the story goes, sold his soul to the devil. Others also believe that the blues died with Stevie Ray Vaughan. But the blues, like many other forms of music, lives on in those who continue to enjoy it, and the places where it finds a home. The faces and the places may change, but the music and the life that it inspired continues to live on. And for many years, the music lived and breathed at the Double Door Inn.

From the outside of the building, there was nothing to indicate that there was anything special on the inside. The building was two stories high, and featured two front doors. Only one of the doors were operable. The plate glass windows were smudged, and a blue neon sign advertised "Live Blues."

Once you entered the Double Door, it might have taken a little time to realize just what an unusual place you had entered. But for those that took the time to look

NICK KARRES, MID 1970s.
Courtesy Double Door Inn archives

through the low lighting, and look at all of the pictures of past performers that surround the walls, it was obvious that the Double Door Inn was the real deal. One could look up at the old wooden rafters of what was at one time an actual family residence. The stage, and stage area was once part of the home's original porch. Well-worn wood surrounded you. The bar, the floors, the stools at the bar. There were advertisements for various brands of beer. Behind the bar, shelves were lined with bottles of different kinds of liquor. There were at least three clocks that were visible if one sat at the bar. The time was never the same on any of them. But the music was always there. To be seen, heard and enjoyed. But no one had any idea that such a place would still exist when it was opened on December 22, 1973. Or, when the house was first built.

"Here's the story that my dad told me," says Matthew Karres about the house. "The house was built in 1911 by a Mr. Wearn, who owned the Wearn Lumber Company. He also lived in the house. At the time, it was called Fox Street, and it was a gravel road. When my dad was a kid, he would walk by that house on his way to Elizabeth Elementary School. When he was in second grade, he had a crush on a little girl that lived in that house."

Charlotte, North Carolina was still a small southern city as the twentieth century began. Largely untouched by the Civil War, the area prospered with the arrival of textiles, and new industries. One of those new businesses was the Wearn Lumber Company, founded by William R. Wearn. Beginning in the early 1900s, the Company soon became one of the most prominent businesses in the Charlotte area. William's brother J. H. Wearn would eventually take the reins of the company, although William continued to stay involved. J. H. Wearn would also buy the Charlotte Hornets baseball team, and build the team a new stadium, which opened as Wearn Field on the corner of Mint and Summit Street in 1908.

By 1911, William Wearn, his wife Fannie, and their children had settled into a large estate on the corner of Elizabeth Avenue and Torrance Street. Torrance was named for the land's previous owner, Stephen Torrance, whom Wearn had bought the land from. Wearn also purchased land that surrounded the estate. Soon after, Fox Street was mapped out and laid down as a gravel road that intersected Elizabeth.

By 1923, The Wearn family was growing, with the birth of William Wearn III.

On December 20th of that same year, William Jr. purchased the land along Fox Street from his parents, and built the home that would later become the Double Door Inn. Tax and deed records do not reveal exactly when the house was built, but 1924 is a safe assumption. The house is listed in the 1930 census at 4 North Fox Street, and would later be renamed 218 North Fox Street in 1935.

Although William Wearn Sr. would die in 1932, the Wearn family held onto their land during the 1930s, and the Wearn family would continue to stay active in Charlotte, with Arthur Wearn serving as Mayor of Charlotte from 1933 to 1935. Wearn decided to run again in 1935, only to discover that his stiffest competition would come from his own neighbor. A native of Iredell County, Ben Douglas had moved to Charlotte from Gastonia in the mid-1920s, and had established a funeral home at the corner of Fox St. and Elizabeth Avenue, right in the middle of the Wearn's homes. Douglas was part of a new wave of businessmen during that time, and decided to run for Mayor against Wearn, a fellow Democrat. Douglas would not only win that election, but go on to serve as Mayor from 1935 until 1941, and later be referred to as being the "Builder Of Modern Day Charlotte."

"They named the airport for him," says Nick Karres about Douglas. "He wanted the city to name Independence Boulevard for him, as well, but they had already named the airport in his honor. Much of the highway cut through land that he owned. I do also have a vague memory of that funeral parlor."

Around this time, William Wearn Jr. made renovations to his home. Fox Street was a busy area during the late 1930s, with numerous homes built on the street during this time. It was probably around this time that the original porch area was walled in, creating what would later be the Double Door's stage area. The house received enough renovations that tax records would later list the house as being built in 1937. By 1945, World War II was slowly coming to to a close, and much of the Elizabeth area of Charlotte had begun to change. The trolleys that ran down Elizabeth Avenue had been replaced by city buses. The Wearn family had sold the Charlotte Hornets, and the former Wearn Field was torn down in 1941. After the passing of his father, William Wearn Jr. began talks with the family's neighbor to sell the family's estate. The front page of the October 2, 1945 edition of the Charlotte Observer confirmed that the Wearn family had sold the estate and adjoining properties to Ben Douglas. "The Wearn property was sold by William R. Wearn Jr. and Robert Morrison Wearn, exectors of the estate of the late

William R. Wearn, founder of the Wearn Lumber Company and long prominent in the business affairs of the city. The property takes up most of the block which is bounded by Elizabeth Avenue, Fox Street, Fifth Street, and Torrence Street. The frontage is 400 feet on Elizabeth Avenue, and 200 feet on Fox. The remainder of East Fifth to Torrence and the whole book of Torrence is included, making almost a city block involved with the deal. The deal involved was understood to be somewhere in the neighborhood of $60,000," reported the Observer. While his own home was not included in the sale to Ben Douglas, Wearn Jr. would pass away just two months later, and his family would sell the house and property to John and Ruth Prather in 1946.

The home would pass through a couple of different hands, before being purchased in 1953 by the Houston family. "The house was bought by a Mrs. Peggy Houston," says Matthew Karres. "Her husband's name was Jake Houston. He was a longtime photographer with the Charlotte Observer. Mrs. Houston was a very good friend of my grandmother's, who lived on Hawthorne Lane. We would go into that house to visit a lot of times, and Jake and his son Charlie were good friends with my father's two younger brothers. They'd served in World War II together, too. Mrs. Houston later decided to sell her business, and Nick's best friend from high school, David Kossade, bought the Lamp Shop. We always had a connection to that house, all of our lives." Peggy and Jake Houston would make numerous renovations to the house during 1953 and 1954, including adding the area that would later became the Double Door's game room.

Brothers Matthew and Nick Karres were born at Presbyterian Hospital. "We have literally been in that neighborhood all of our lives," says Nick. "I went to Park Road Elementary, Sedgfield Elementary, and Myers Park High. I then went to UNC-Chapel hill, came back here very soon after, and started working.

"I was with a real estate company, at the time. I wasn't sure what I wanted to do. I am an independent sort. I did a couple interviews, and I wondered, 'What an I doing here?' I knew that I was going to do something here myself. I was active in athletics, and met a lot of people. You could go anywhere back then, and see somebody you knew."

In 1973, gasoline prices were quickly escalating and had hit $1.00 a gallon, and the economy was in a recession. Interest rates were at a historic high. Into this,

Nick Karres, two years removed from his graduation from UNC-Chapel Hill, was working for a local real estate company. With the economic conditions of the time, the job was a challenge. One of his assignments was to try and find a business to lease the building at 218 Independence Boulevard that had recently been vacated when the Peggy Houston Lamp Shop relocated.

"I kept trying to lease this building, but everything kept falling through," Nick would later recall. "Interest rates made it difficult to find a business willing to lease the space. At the time, there were very few places in Charlotte where young people could go to hang out and perhaps drink a beer. So I began to consider opening a small bar in the building. My older brother, Matthew had some experience in the business, so I consulted with him about the possibilities. I almost literally begged him to go into this business with me. I knew that I wanted a family member involved, should I start a business."

"I had worked in bars in Chapel Hill and Charlotte, but I was not sure that I wanted to be involved in actually owning such a business," remembers Matthew Karres. "Have you heard of Zach Galifianakis? My first job was tending bar for his grandparents, in Chapel Hill. I had several concerns ranging from the actual location that Nick had in mind to whether or not we would be able to secure an ABC (Alcohol Beverage Control) permit to sell beer." But after much discussion about the possibilities, the brothers decided that they would open a small bar in the building.

"I had another job that offered me a management job, and I turned it down, because we were renovating the Double Door," adds Matthew. "I told Nick that we would have two problems. With all of those rooms, they probably won't give us a beer license. You're gonna have a heck of a parking problem. But I thought about it, and I thought, 'Well, I'll either be bartending for somebody else, or this could be a real opportunity.'"

By 1973, the road had become a major highway known as Independence Boulevard, very near the center of the downtown district. Central Piedmont Community College, which was founded in 1963 on the former campus of Central High, and Charlotte College (now known as UNC-Charlotte) was located just across the street. Behind the building, there was a sizable community where many younger people lived due to the low rents for apartments and houses, and the close proximity to the community college.

Since both of the Karres brothers were fairly recent college graduates, neither had a lot of money. They discussed the situation with their parents, James and Georgia. "They were not really impressed with our idea," remembers Nick. "They had concerns about what problems we might encounter with such a business. Operating a business that served alcohol in the Bible Belt was a somewhat radical idea at the time." Eventually, their father agreed to loan them $10,000 to start the business. He also took photos of the building for inventory purposes, providing some of the earliest photos taken at the Double Door.

"My parents helped a lot," adds Matthew Karres. "My dad came in and painted the place. He painted a lot of the furniture. We opened that bar spending less than $10,000. Try to open today on less than $10,000."

"It took way too long," Nick would later say about preparing the Double Door to be a bar. "Although I knew a lot of people in Charlotte, I didn't know any builders. My dad knew this guy, Harry Lainis, and he built the first bar. John Zachodzki, and Jon Mullis, who was also a musician, did the carpentry work. I entered that building around August and September to start work on it. I would just go in and putz around, because I was figuring it out. But then again, in that building we were in uncharted territory. Nobody had really turned a house into a bar, yet. You've got all of this change of use with zoning, and then the building inspectors. The first inspector that came in said, "Have you signed this lease? You may not want to do what you want to do." I remember thinking, am I supposed to slip him a $100 bill. Tell me what I have to do, and I'll do it. The furnace was old, so I got the owner of the building to put in a new furnace, and put sheet rock around it. We couldn't use the upstairs. Initially, I had to close both entrances, because there was an entrance on the back. So I said, "That's not feasible for me to do that. So we closed the back door, and put sheet rock up on both sides of the front door, and I was able to go [upstairs] that way. So we could use the upstairs that way, and nobody knew the difference. Just bringing it up to code."

"We knocked down a lot of walls, recalls Matthew Karres. "Originally, along the side of the stage, there was a fireplace. We had to take that down. There was a lot of remodeling done from the original house. It took two or three months. You have to wait on the inspectors.

"We also paid off that building fast. That's one of the reasons why it was there for so long. If we'd had to be paying Charlotte rents, I guarantee that the Double Door would've been gone a long time ago."

Finding an appropriate name for the new business proved to be another concern. "Back then, no one thought it just being a bar, because there wasn't just a bar," remembers Nick Karres. "So I was thinking about some kind of theme, and I thought about decorating it with a western theme, like a saloon. And that's what I did at first. I got one of those catalogs from Jack Daniel's, and I ordered a few posters out of that. Some of the early t-shirts look like that. One night, I was watching a movie, and they named their bar The Double Eagle. And that got me thinking."

Nick and Matthew's mom would soon provide the final idea. "I remember discussing our quandary one evening at dinner with our parents," says Matthew. "Our mother looked thoughtful for a moment, and then in a matter of fact way, said the place has two doors. 'Why don't you call it the Double Door?' This sounded logical to the two of us and resulted in us naming the business the Double Door Inn."

"We just opened as a place for people to come. Originally, the bar was quite small," Nick would later say. "You could come into the bar, turn left and go through the kitchen, and be all the way around. When customers first entered, there was a large window that opened into the bar.

"The first night, we gave away a keg of beer. First night, come on in, there's a keg of free beer. Back then, when you walked in, you could go left into the door, and take you into what later became our kitchen. It wasn't a kitchen back then. We had pinball machines. You could walk around the building. You'd then go out of that room, into the original men's bathroom. That later became the first thing that we fixed. You would then go into what later became the staff room. We had a couple of foosball tables in there. Instead of going upstairs, you could walk straight through the into the main room. We later closed that opening. You could walk in, turn left, and walk through in a circle. It was kind of cool. We had booths in the main room. Maybe about 50, 60 people that night. The second night, I don't remember."

When the Double Door opened, there were very few bars in Charlotte. One of the others, and perhaps the most popular, was The Pullout, which was located at

South Boulevard and Tremont. "That was the only other club in town, remembers Nick. "They had food upstairs, and games downstairs. And that place was doing great. The owner was kind of a crazy guy. Something happened, and a couple of their bartenders started hanging out at the Double Door. And then, they started telling other people. And suddenly, it was like the floodgates opened, and we were really busy for a while."

While Nick and Matthew continued to work all the time at the bar, they began to seek help from others. "Dennis Martin was our first daytime employee, and then we had Mike Payne working at night. Our first bartenders actually were women. Debbie Ansbach and Cindy Bayer. Debbie was the first one. When I was hiring her, I didn't know what to do, because I'd never hired anyone before. The bar was originally square, and you would move around it. It was pretty crazy, too. We had some creatures in there. People would play games like crazy. We added foosball tables. People would line up to play the video games. We did good business with that."

Even before the Double Door officially opened its doors, it had already caught the interest of several young musicians in the area. "I went in there about a week before the place really opened and had a beer and talked to Nick," says Jake Berger. "I remember that before they started having live music, the bar was quite small. Where the kitchen [was later] was then the game room. You could walk in, walk around, go upstairs and when you came down you would be in the game room. It was weird. It was just an old house."

One of the first official regulars at the bar was Travis, a Korean War veteran that lived nearby. During the first few years, he spent many an afternoon hanging around and expressing his opinion on just about everything as he sipped from a can of Pabst Blue Ribbon beer. He met a cook named Virginia, who was employed at a nearby restaurant and frequently walked with her to her job, and then back to the Double Door. When they decided to get married in late 1974, the natural place for the ceremony was the bar. Neil Hamlin, who had a mail order credential to practice as a minister, officiated at the ceremony. Later, there was a reception complete with wedding cake, and the event was covered by the Charlotte Observer, the first time that the local daily paper covered the still-fledgling bar.

ORIGINAL SEATING AREA OF THE CLUB, MID 1970S.
Courtesy Double Door Inn archives

ORIGINAL FRONT AREA OF THE CLUB.
Courtesy Double Door Inn archives

Nick and Matthew Karres were happy to see the coverage that the wedding got. Especially since it was for something other than the rowdy reputation that the bar was earning. "The Double Door was really bad, at first," says Matthew Karres. "The drinking age was 18. It was the tail end of the Vietnam War, so a lot of people were going to school on the GI Bill. A lot of these guys, their wives would drop them off at school while they were going to work, then they'd pick them up after work. These guys weren't in class more than a couple of hours, so they spent the rest of their time at the Double Door.

"We didn't have liquor by the drink. We had what we called Brown Bagging. The reason that we put in music was because of the fights that we were having in there. It was terrible. I can't remember if it was the fourth or fifth Friday night, and I said, 'Damn, we have a fight in here every Friday night.' I started counting from that night. We went 54 straight Fridays that we had a fight. It was like The Jerry Springer Show. Saturday night, you had a 50/50 chance of a fight. Always on Friday night. We had a guy fire on a police helicopter one night. It was rough.

"One thing that saved us was that Nick was a jock. He'd gotten a football scholarship from Chapel Hill, and he was the state discus and shotput championship, and he had the state record, as well. And he could fight. I only saw one guy come back for seconds. Nick knocked him down again, and the guy got up, and just went 'Ah!' Waved him off, gave up and walked out. It was the funniest thing I'd ever seen."

Other groups were not as easy to send away. "The Outlaws started coming into the bar, and we didn't want them in there," says Matthew Karres. "So we told them that they couldn't come in with their colors on. And they took umbrage at that. They said, 'We like this bar. The days of tearing a place up are over. We're going to sue you for discrimination, and we're going to own this bar.' Their lawyer was a guy named Mike Plumides. He had a brother named Johnny, they shared a law office together. My grandfather was best man at John Plumides' father's wedding. My dad was best man at John's wedding. We did all of our real estate closings through them. Mike Plumides was also the lawyer for the Outlaws. So the Outlaws went into his office, and he said, 'Look, those guys are very good friends of mine, and my family. Do me a favor and find another bar to pick on. Just go in without your colors and have a good time.' And they left us alone after that."
"I don't remember it that way," counters Nick Karres. 'I remember that Concerned Bikers Of Charlotte came in, and said, "Can we meet here, once or twice a

month?' I said, sure. I would have, even today. But that caught the attention of the Outlaws, who came in a couple of times with their colors on. We had a friend of ours named John Voss, who would sometimes be at the front door. He was one of those guys that could talk to anybody. We knew that [the Outlaws] were coming in. John was waiting out in front, and talked to them. After that, they came back in, but they took their colors off."

One of the better things that did bring people to the Double Door around this time was their variety of foods, and priced for hungry students and characters. "If you look at our early menus," says Matthew Karres. "Hot dogs were 50 cents. Hoagies were a dollar."

The Double Door was also offering other things that couldn't be found in Charlotte during that time. "We sold bagels," says Nick. "Nobody sold bagels back then. In Charlotte, in 1975? We had lots of bagels.

"That was a little too New York Cityish for people in Charlotte, at the time," adds Matthew.

"People would come over from the school, and say, 'Do you have anything to eat?' 'So we just threw together food," says Nick. "That's where Basil Coston, being a daytime guy, he could bring in different things. That's when we had booths along the wall. I remember planning those menus, thinking that were going to get into food, but then we started to do music. And suddenly, there's 200 people in your place, and there's like a thousand cigarette butts on the floor, and you have to clean up and turn it around by the next day to serve food, and it was hard to do all of that." While the bar would eventually move away from being a full-fledged restaurant continued to serve food at the bar throughout the day up until its final years.

Mike Martin started working at the Double Door in 1975. "I began working on a part-time basis. I had been coming here as a customer frequently enough that I had gotten to know both Nick and Matt," Martin remembered. "One day, I happened to be around and heard someone mention needing to take some time off for vacation. Nick knew that I was working already part-time at the Yellow Rose Tavern, so he asked me if I wanted to fill in. I took him up on the request."

Martin, and George Mandrapilias, who was hired soon after Martin carved out the trend for those at the Double Door. If you worked there, you were there for a long time. Many of the Double Door's employees would go on to work there for 15, 20, 30 years or more. Mandrapilias would go on to tend bar at the Double Door for 33 years, while Martin will still tending bar when it closed in January of 2017.

"Nick and Matt, we all grew up together," says Mandrapilias. "It was a tight-knit Greek community. I went to Western [Carolina], and came back in February of 1976, and was just piddling around. And my mom saw Nick at church one day, and Nick asked mom what I was doing. So I went to talk to Nick, and I started working there the next month."

Martin started working in the kitchen when the venue used to sell pizza and had its own pizza oven. "Joe Smothers and I used to make and sell pizzas, box after box during that time, and then eventually, I also began working behind the bar slinging beers. As I began to get more hours here, this became my primary job."

When asked about his some of his most memorable shows, "I can remember especially when Luther Allison played here. The show started with his back-up band who played several numbers. Just as the crowd got a little restless, I heard an almost thunderous noise from the front staircase. I looked up and sure enough, here came Allison down the steps, playing his guitar and wandering through the packed crowd to the stage. Once he hit the stage, the band played straight through for more than two and a half hours. The audience didn't even ask for an encore. Everyone was so blown away by the show that they were almost stunned. I do remember the guys in the band had to almost run to the men's room. After sipping water all night and playing so long, they definitely had to go!

"To me, Nick is one of the main reasons that I stuck around. No matter what things I might have done incorrectly, he always was there, and offered sometimes fatherly advice but because of him, it became worthwhile to stay. I had the opportunity to later go on to UNCC and earn my B.A. degree and even took some graduate courses due to the flexible hours that I worked. When my son played T-ball and soccer, I was always there. I even had the time to coach some of his teams and had I been working more traditional hours, I would never have been able to have done all of those things as well as earn a living.

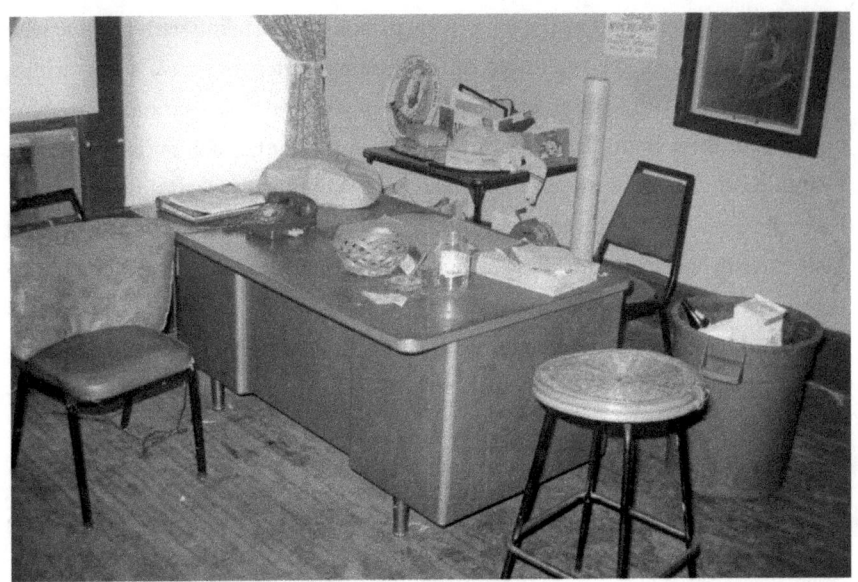

NICK KARRES' OFFICE, 1970s.
Courtesy Double Door Inn archives

GAME ROOM, 1970s.
Courtesy Double Door Inn archives

"Probably the worst part of the job for me personally is dealing with patrons who may be very nice in the beginning of the evening. After they have a few drinks, personalities often change and the same person who was very nice and easy-going only two or three hours ago, may turn into an unpleasant, loud obnoxious person. I often have to remind myself that I have some complicity when this happens as I am the person who served them the alcohol. Sometimes, it is difficult to deal with their behavior, yet knowing that I was the one who served them, I have to stay in control of my own feelings. We are taught to watch customers for the signs of overindulgence but it can be very difficult to spot, especially on a busy evening when orders are coming in from all sides.

"The reputation of this business was built by providing good music, good service and cold beer," adds Martin. "Many of those who came in had the feeling of being at home, sort of like a neighborhood pub."

Throughout the 1970s, there was a small building located alongside the Double Door, with the unforgettable title of Chronosynclasticinfidibulum. Originally, the building had been a Toddle House restaurant. It was then converted into what was known among the hippie countercultural types as a head shop. "Head shops," for those who may not be aware, generally cater to people who are looking for alternative merchandise such as pipes, rolling papers and other supplies necessary for those who partake of marijuana.

"We worked hard to dispel that we were a rough place. I wanted businessmen to be able to come in and have a beer next to anybody. Blue collar, white collar, whatever."

Woody Mitchell, a local writer and musician, was among those early Double Door patrons. "In the early going, the Double Door was the neighborhood hangout for the area of the Elizabeth neighborhood around the now defunct Stanley's Drug store, where counter-cultural types could get all the necessities of life. Rent in the area was absurdly cheap then, and a lot of musicians, artists, and other assorted oddballs shared the old houses and apartments, forming a loose community that naturally gravitated to what we called The Bar.

"People started bringing their acoustic guitars in and sitting around on barstools singing songs everybody knew or ones they had just written. The late Jon Mullis was the ring-leader, and I recall Michael Brett, Jack Lawrence, Davey Long and Jim Nicholson chiming in at various times, plus many others."

Other musicians that would later be a part of the venue's history had also begun to visit. "I had come back to Charlotte after being away for several years, and my girlfriend at the time suggested we go there," says Pat Walters. "It was laid back. Comfortable. There wasn't a stage then. I vaguely remember pinball machines, foosball and pool tables."

The first live music was performed in what became the game room. One of their friends, Tim Beaver, installed red and black carpet and those who wanted to listen to the music paid 25 or 50 cents to be admitted to the area and sit on the floor. The first musician who performed was Wayne Erbsen, a guitar and banjo player. "I always say that Wayne was the first, and that Lenny Federal was the second," says Nick. "Wayne had the professional name, because he had played all of these places, and he was a music teacher. So when he asked about playing there, it was more of a serious thing. So we started doing shows in the back room. And once we started doing that, it was all over."

He was followed by many eager local musicians including Jon Mullis, Michael Brett, Lenny Federal and others too numerous to mention. The success of this early attempt to provide an inviting atmosphere where one could relax with friends, hang out, and actually listen to live music is probably one of the cornerstones of what became the Charlotte live music scene."

"As new bars began to open, I could see the fickle nature of the business," adds Nick. "We began to see that if we planned on being here for awhile, we needed to make a decision. Our need for something different to draw customers on a more regular basis coincided with the need for a place for local musicians to play."

"The cover charge took care of a lot of the riff raff," says Matthew Karres. "We knew a lot of those musicians. We were neighbors with the Duckworth's, and Zan McLeod."

"At some point it dawned on Nick that he could draw a crowd if he actually staged musical events," says Woody Mitchell. "It was all acoustic at first, and being an electric guitar guy, I didn't play there much except to sit in on acoustic occasionally with Jon or whomever. In 1974, John Wicker and I cranked up a band called Paradox, playing a rocking blend of the esoteric and the nutty. Somehow, we talked Nick into trying electric music, and it went over well. To my knowledge, we were the first electric band to play the Double Door.

"By the next year, Lenny Federal and I had joined forces in the Renegade Blues Band. We played Lenny's spirited folk-rock, my raunchy blues-based stuff, and this new music roaring out of Jamaica, reggae. By this time, the Double Door was bringing in local bands every weekend for a two-night stand, with Davey Long doing the booking. There wasn't an actual stage. They'd clear out the area where the stage is now and we'd set up on the floor against the front wall."

"When they first started having acoustic music, it was located in the back room that is now the game room," remembers Berger. "Lenny Federal was one of the first acoustic guitarists that I saw play there. There was no sound equipment and there was just a corner for the band to stand and play for the audience that was often seated on the floor. I remember the band that Lenny and Woody had called the Renegade Blues Band. They played the first reggae song that I ever heard, and they were quite good."

Although his bands and accompanying players changed over the years, Lenny Federal would keep returning to the venue, right up to its final night. Some of the other names that his bands claimed were Lenny Don't Surf, The Buddy-Ro Band, The Federal Brothers, and the almost infamous Federal Bureau of Rock & Roll. The FBR&R, as they were often referred to, played many Sunday nights as the house band. It was quite a well-known event. Not much was open on a Sunday night and many of the regulars at these shows referred to it as going to Sunday services.

There were many different musicians who played with Lenny, a guitar virtuoso who once described himself as a "guitar-wrestler." Some of those included Jack Lawrence (who went to play guitar for many years with Doc Watson), Bill Walpole, Wendell Elliott, Mahlon Thomas, Lenny's brother Michael Federal, and many others. Lenny had the reputation as being very supportive of the music scene, and spent many evenings sharing his talents with the crowd at the bar. Dave Long would later describes Lenny as "setting the standard for musicians who followed. He is an absolutely remarkable guitar player and I feel that he is just as good as

ORIGINAL DOUBLE DOOR INN AD, CIRCA 1974.
Courtesy Double Door Inn archives

CHRONOSYNCLASTICINFINDIBULUM, ORIGINAL BUILDING NEXT DOOR TO THE DOUBLE DOOR INN, MID 1970s.
Courtesy Double Door Inn archives

almost anyone who has ever graced the Double Door stage."

Rob Thorne, longtime drummer of the Spongetones, recalls the atmosphere that surrounded the Double Door during that time. "The first time I went to the Double Door, it was just a beer joint. Just a bar, a local watering hole. Then they started having live acoustic music with Jon Mullis and other players. The live music at the venue was strictly acoustic. Davey Long often played with [Jon] Mullis, as well. All of the players at that point in time had come out of the folk music scene and the Double Door was a perfect place for them to play to live audiences."

"Nick wasn't letting grass grow under his feet, though," adds Mitchell. "He decided to take the plunge and hire a name from out of town, hoping people would pay a cover charge to hear good entertainment. Davey booked Larry Jon Wilson, who was known as one of the outlaw country music singer/ songwriters, and hailed from Augusta, Georgia. To everyone's delight and relief, listeners showed up in droves. Jon Mullis opened the show, with Karen Deane on vocals and me on acoustic lead. Larry Jon won the crowd over and got a great response. For the final tune of the night, he got Jon, Karen and me up to sing harmonies on 'Geronimo's Cadillac.' A real Kodak moment."

"Dave Long did a lot for us," Matthew Karres would later say. "He was our first booking agent." Another popular North Carolina band, Arrogance, also played the Double Door during this time. By this time, the musicians had also moved from the back room, to setting up in the front of the bar. The success of these shows became a launching pad for an even bigger show.

The circumstances for what would become the Double Door's first major booking has since passed into legend. Dave Long would later recount it this way. "Steve Nichols was driving to work at Reliable Music, and he sees these two hippies hitchhiking beside the road. He picks 'em up and they ask, 'We're going to Reliable Music. Do you know where that is?' Steve said, 'I'm going there!' Turns out they were members of the Dregs, looking for a bass. They'd flown in on [Dixie Dregs lead guitarist] Steve Morse's private plane and hitchhiked from the airport. The guys asked Steve [Nichols] if there's anywhere to play in town, and Steve said sure. The Double Door Inn!"

"I don't recall that story at all," Nick Karres would later say. "What I remember

PATRONS AT THE BAR, 1970s.
Courtesy Double Door Inn archives

ORIGINAL SPACE LEADING FROM BACK ROOM OF
DOUBLE DOOR INN. Courtesy Double Door Inn archives

TRAVIS' WEDDING, 1975.
Courtesy Double Door Inn archives

is that Dave Long came to me and said, "Let's book this band called the Dixie Dregs.' So I said, 'Okay, let's do it.'"

No matter what the truth is, Long was able to book the Dixie Dregs for two nights at the Double Door in June of 1976. After the show was booked, Nick Karres realized that another change was in order. "We started thinking," says Nick, "This is gonna be a big show. We should have a stage. So we built one." The stage that Nick and his friends built for the Dregs show would become the platform that every musician would use for the next forty years.

"They pulled up in a little trailer," remembers Nick. "We paid them 300 bucks." "[The Dixie Dregs] had the most gear on stage that I've ever seen," Matthew Karres would later say about the band's two-night stand at the venue.

"Once the Dixie Dregs played here and I heard such a wonderful band live in an intimate setting, I was hooked," Nick Karres would later remember. "The music began to be the most important reason to keep going, at least for me."

"I saw the Dixie Dregs there," says Rob Thorne. "By that time, no other bar was doing what the Karres brothers were doing. There was no other place to play in Charlotte. Every other bar in town was hiring cover bands that played Top Forty hits, or else they were strictly into country or R&B. Initially, it was pretty loosely organized. You could just sit in with people and play. It was good for an audience. They always knew they were going to hear some good live music."

For blues music, the Double Door Inn came along at a time when the genre was in search of a new home. Despite a resurgence in blues-based music during the late 1960s, many blues musicians had seen their fan base fade by 1973. The variety of idea and music genres had given way to folk music, country-rock and pop. It would took another wave of musicians, and venues like the Double Door to bring it back to larger audiences.

"By the time the Double Door opened," Jake Berger once observed, "most people were listening to what they could hear on the radio. Some of the great soul music greats had passed on, and the blues was definitely in a decline. No one listened to that music at all. I believe that it was guys like Nick who helped Blues music survive until it got healthy again."

Mac Arnold, a left-handed bass player who hails from Greenville, South Carolina, played with the Muddy Waters Blues band from 1966 to 1967. "I remember those old days. I was still a young man but I traveled with the band all over the country. Muddy had two black Cadillacs and that was the way we got from gig to gig. It was quite difficult as it cost money to travel and most of our gigs did not pay that much." Arnold would leave the Waters band in 1967, and return home to South Carolina. It would another thirty years before Arnold returned to the stage, playing the Double Door and other venues throughout the Southeast United States.

Throughout the 1970s, Slowly, another generation began to pick up and carry on the music. New artists began to build a touring base throughout the East Coast, and other parts of the United States. Independent record labels, such as the Chicago-based Alligator Records, began to release records by Hound Dog Taylor, Albert Collins and and many others. Many of these artists would soon begin to make regular appearances at the the Double Door Inn.

Soon after their show at the Double Door, the Dixie Dregs shared a bill with a band that would change the future of the venue. "The Dregs often played with the Nighthawks from Washington, DC, and told them about our venue," adds Nick Karres. "The Nighthawks were immensely popular in the DC area, and they frequently passed through the Charlotte area on their tour to play in places like Atlanta, but previously had found no place to play anywhere near this location."

The Nighthawks originally band formed in the spring of 1972 in the Washington, DC area. By the late 1970s, they played frequently with the Dixie Dregs and had opened for several legendary blues acts, including Muddy Waters. At that time, there were two main circuits that traveling bands followed in order to get the most gigs as possible along the way. The Nighthawks generally traveled from somewhere around Boston to Atlanta, stopping for gigs along the way. "I've known Nick for nearly 40 years and he is just a great guy," says founding Nighthawks member Mark Wenner. "Nick has always been kind, considerate and honest in all of his dealings with my band."

"The first time that I saw the Nighthawks," says George Mandrapilias, "I was like, 'Oh my God! Who are you guys?' They're the only band that I went out and bought all of their records. It cost me about two night's worth of pay."

The Nighthawks' first show at the Double Door brought a packed audience. "At the time, the Nighthawks were doing some shows with Gregg Allman," recalls Nick. "Rolling Stone had just done an article about him playing with the Nighthawks, so a lot of people showed up that night to see if Gregg was playing with them. He wasn't, but they put on a great show."

After the initial show, Nighthawks harmonica player and longtime leader Mark Wenner approached Nick with a list of bands. "He gave me a piece of paper with a list of twelve bands. He said, 'This is who you should book. If they call, answer the phone.'" Most of the bands on the list played some form of blues music, and this was probably one of the reasons that the Double Door became a well-known venue for those who were fans of blues music. Some of the bands on that list were Roomful Of Blues, The Fabulous Thunderbirds, Catfish Hodge, and Skip Castro. Another name on that list was Robert Lockwood Jr. (or Robert Jr. Lockwood, as he was sometimes billed), who had learned to play the guitar with the help of his onetime stepfather, Robert Johnson.

In the months soon after that first Nighthawks show, word about the Double Door Inn, as both a neighborhood hangout as well as a blues venue began to spread. It had led to many nights of incredible music, camaraderie, an occasional drunk or two but all in all, most things were going pretty well for the business. Many local bands were starting to coalesce, playing gigs around the area including the Double Door. There were many nights when it was quite literally shoulder to shoulder, bodies packed together in the old house and always the music ringing out above the din.

"The crowds were crazy," recalls Woody Mitchell. "Everybody came early and stayed late. By this time, Nick had put in an actual stage, but the bar hadn't been pushed back to extend the room yet. Everybody was crammed into the space between the big columns and the west wall. Looking toward the back of the room from the stage, through a turgid cloud of tobacco smoke as thick as a London fog, all you could see was people, occupying every square inch of space. George [Mandrapilias] and Martino [Mike Martin] were whirling dervishes behind the bar, slinging beers out as fast as people could pay for them. No liquor then, it was still against the law to sell it in a club."

Another popular feature of the Double Door throughout the 1970s, and into the

MIKE (EMPLOYED SINCE 1975) TENDING BAR, JUNE 2008.
Photo by Daniel Coston

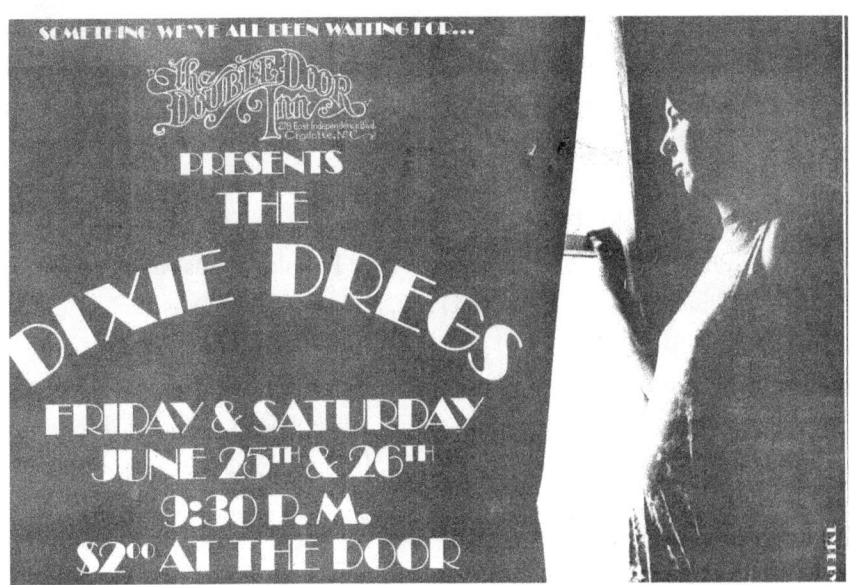
DIXIE DREGS SHOW FLYER, 1976.
Courtesy Double Door Inn archives

1980s, was their game room. The area had once been a showcase space for the Peggy Houston Lamp Shop, with multiple electrical outlets. These outlets would get a lot of use with the most popular features during the venue's early days, video games.

"We had Pong", says Nick. "It had just came out. We were the first in town to have that. That was really popular."

"The video games were really popular," adds Matthew. "As soon as they raised the drinking age to 21, people weren't playing the video games anymore, they phased them out in the 90s. We had a good working relationship with the company that handled those machines. They put in the machines. If a machine wasn't doing as well, they would move the machines around to different locations. They took 10 percent off the top, then it was a 50-50 split from then on."

"I shouldn't admit this," adds George Mandrapilias, "But sometimes, we would play video games until the sun came up."

Nationally known acts, and local acts were filling at the Double Door with more frequency by this time. This included Sam & Dave, the famous Stax Records duo. Despite touring without original singer Sam Moore, they put on quite a show, filling the stage with a full band, including a horn section. Many times, these and other bands were booked for Friday and Saturday nights and packed the place on both nights.

"I first played there with The Stanleyville Rhythm Section which included David Floyd and Phil Lowe," says Pat Walters. "Bobby Donaldson was on the early gigs, as well. The lineup later became me, David, Phil and Debby Dobbins."

"I first played there in 1978, with the James Hoover Group," adds Jamie Hoover. The next time was would have been playing keyboards with the Moore & Perrin Band. It was a cool place. I was a kid. It smelled like beer and puke, all of the things I loved.

"The Moore & Perrin Band was a fabulous band. Me, Joyous Perrin, Carolyn Moore and Jim Brock. With my band, I know that we were the first band to play punk rock at the Double Door. We played 'Sheena Is A Punk Rocker', 'White

NICK KARRES UPSTAIRS WITH MARK WENNER AND JIMMY THACKERY OF THE NIGHTHAWKS, 1978.
Photo by Pat Shanklin/Double Door archives

DOUBLE DOOR INN SOFTBALL TEAM WITH THEIR TOURNAMENT TROPHY, 1975. Standing left to right, Doug McRae, Nick Karres, Dennis Martin, Tom Tate, Mike Payne, Terch Whitesides, Cam McRae. Kneeling left to right, Mike Cassel, Jim Morris, Lenny Federal.
Courtesy Double Door Inn archives

Punks On Dope' by the Tubes, and 'Psycho Killer,' by the Talking Heads."

After the Nighthawks had first played at the Double Door in the mid-seventies, the club was able to book The Fabulous Thunderbirds, out of Austin, Texas. Guitarist Jimmie Vaughan and singer-harmonica player Kim Wilson led the band that was one of the first blues-based bands to come out of the Austin blues scene. The Thunderbirds formed in 1974 but did not release an album until 1979. The real breakthrough for this band came in 1986 with the release of the song "Tuff Enuff." This song made it into the Top Ten of the Billboard pop charts, by which time the Thunderbirds had played the Double Door stage numerous times.

But it was Jimmie Vaughan's younger brother who would go on to revitalize the national blues scene. In 1972, Stevie Ray Vaughan joined a band known as the Nightcrawlers. Later, he formed a blues-rock group with singer Lou Ann Barton that went by the name Triple Threat Revue. In 1978, after the departure of Barton from the group, Vaughan renamed his band, Double Trouble. This is the band that first played at the Double Door for two nights in the fall of 1979.

More and more alliances were beginning to build among regular patrons and there was often a party atmosphere in the parking lot after the shows. Mookie Brill, a talented bass player and winner of two Blues Music Awards (the Grammys of the blues world), remembers being a young guy who attended many of the shows, and was fortunate enough to often hang out for awhile after the show. "We would just sit out on the cars and shoot the shit," he remembers. Sometimes these impromptu gatherings would last late into the night.

"The first time I saw Stevie Ray Vaughan was there, and it was in October, 1979," Brill adds. "The band was called Double Trouble and they were scheduled for a two-day weekend. I went in there and I was just knocked out by Stevie. I thought, 'This guy's going to be huge one day.' In fact, when they were knocking out the old bathrooms, there was a towel rack and someone had broken the mirror and on the cardboard underneath, Stevie Ray had signed his autograph. At the time, no one knew how big he was going to be some day so I took it. In fact, I still have it. It's a completely different signature than the one he used later on."

"There might not have been twenty people there, the first time he played," recalls George Mandrapilias. "After he played and left, I remember thinking, 'Man,

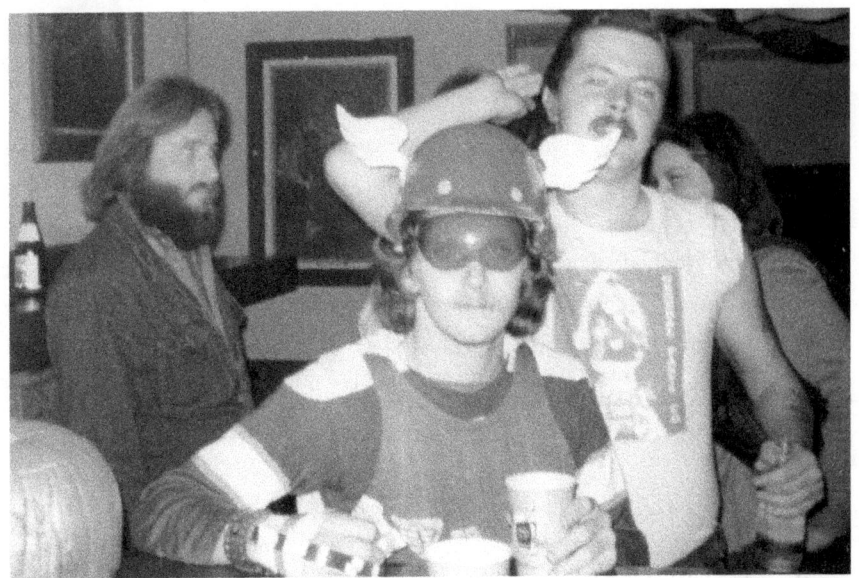

LENNY FEDERAL, HALLOWEEN 1975.
Photo by Debbie Shott.

SHELIA CARLISLE OF ARHOOLY, LATE 1970s.
Courtesy Double Door Inn archives

what's the matter with us?' Seeing and hearing him, and not realizing how great he was until much later."

"I remember [show promoter] Jo Dawkins introducing me to Stevie Ray Vaughan in the dressing room," remembers Scott Cable, who began attending the Double Door during this time. "She said, 'Scott, this is the incredible Stevie Vaughan.' Stevie kind of looked at the floor and said, 'Aww, I ain't that good.' We hung for awhile and talked. He was a real nice guy. Jo called me the next day to see if they could stay at my place as they couldn't afford a room for the night." Vaughan, and Double Trouble would go on to play the Double Door three more times between 1979 and 1982.

"I remember that they were taking down their gear after the show," Matthew Karres would later recall about Stevie Ray Vaughan's first show, "and he laid out on the bar, and I don't know how he got his head underneath the draft spicket, and he said, "Turn it on." I turned it on, and he started chug-a-lugging right out of the the spicket. I thought that he was gonna kill himself."

"Touring bands would come through, and be so cool and accessible," remembered Scott Cable, who attended a lot of shows at the Double Door during this time. "They were happy to have whatever crowd came and after gigs, Mookie, myself, and others would often hang with bands in the parking lot. We often listened to cassettes of whatever we had. Big Walter, Magic Sam, the Fabulous Thunderbirds, Chicago Bob Nelson, Eddie Shaw, and others. The Legendary Blues Band with Pinetop Perkins were all open and friendly, just talking and drinking beer with us. At the age of seventeen, these guys were like huge stars to me and some of them could not always afford hotel rooms. Often bands would crash at my house to save money. My mom and dad would wake up to sometimes find six or seven guys passed out in the living room. The Double Door opened a lot of doors for us."

"I was also there when [legendary blues musician and songwriter] Willie Dixon played in 1984," Brill would later remember. "At that time he was still bringing the bass fiddle out. He would do three or four songs on the fiddle and then he would sing. His sons were in the band along with Carey Bell, and Chico Chism on the drums." Brill has traveled around the world playing music but when asked how it felt to come back and play on the stage in the Double Door, "It's like going back in the living room!" he says. "I used to live around the corner from there for

MARK WENNER OF THE NIGHTHAWKS POINTING TO HIS BAND'S NAME ON THE GREEN ROOM WALL, APRIL 2008. Photo by Daniel Coston.

STAGE AREA OF DOUBLE DOOR INN, CIRCA LATE 1970s.
Courtesy Double Door Inn archives

more than ten years, so it was sort of like my living room. In fact, Nick was the one who gave me the name Mookie. He thought I looked like Ed 'Kookie' Burns, on Sunset Strip."

"The Double Door Inn is where I first met Carey Bell," Cable also recalled. "Who knew I would end up being his band leader some fifteen years later? I was always the youngster in the crowd. I grew a goatee to try and look older, but it didn't really work. I was not a very good guitar player back then. Mookie [Brill] had been playing awhile by the time I started hanging around, but bands were gracious and let me sit in even though I was pretty bad."

Three days before Stevie Ray Vaughan's first appearance, Karres booked a new group of local musicians for their first show at the Double Door Inn. Their original lineup, Jake Berger, Pat Walters, Steve Stoeckel and Rob Thorne, had been playing for years in a variety of groups. This new lineup bonded over a love of the Beatles, and 1960s British Invasion music. Berger had suggested the joking name of the Spongetones, and they kept it. After the band's first ever gig at another bar, The Hitchin' Post, Karres welcomed the band to the Double Door for the first time. It would not be their last.

"If you had a project or new band, Nick was open to giving you a spot," Pat Walters would later recall. "In the late 70's I played every Sunday night at the Double Door with The Steve Jones Quartet for about two years, so I knew Nick and the DD crew pretty well. Steve Stoeckel and I had started getting together over the summer of 1979 to learn our favorite Beatle and 60's British Invasion tunes. We rehearsed a bit with Rob Thorne and Jake Berger, and were ready to go!"

"It gave us a chance to formulate what we were all about, and people just ate it up," Rob Thorne would later say.

"I called the entertainment writer at the Charlotte Observer and told about our gig, and we got a little write-up, which helped get a crowd. Nobody was playing what we were at the time", adds Pat Walters. "A very nice moment was on that first gig in '79, we played "If I Fell", a Beatles song from A Hard Day's Night. I think the whole room was swaying and everyone had these huge smiles on their faces. Putting it in perspective, it had been fifteen years since A Hard Day's Night. Nobody was playing The Beatles and others of their era live, and if they did it,

SAM & DAVE, 1978.
Courtesy Double Door Inn archives

they didn't do it right. The crowd was people in their twenties that were around when the British Invasion happened and they were people that loved that music and were ready to hear it again, live. We just wanted to play the music, and didn't considered it as a commercial situation."

Other genres of music began to find homes at the Double Door as the 1970s drew to a close. Awareness Arts Ensemble brought reggae music to Charlotte for the first time, while zydeco music by bands such as Nathan and the Zydeco Cha-Chas, and future Grammy winner Terence Simien And His Zydeco Band also began to make regular appearances at the venue. But it was blues music that attract musicians from around the world to the Double Door Inn.

Originally from Massachusetts, Bob Margolin played in the Muddy Waters Blues Band during the years 1973 to 1980, and can be seen standing behind Waters in the legendary movie, The Last Waltz. "By late 1979 I could see that I would soon be starting my own band," remembers Margolin. "During a time when Muddy was off, a friend of mine who lived in Washington, DC but was from North Carolina booked some NC dates for me. One of them was the Double Door in the fall of 1979."

"I think it's significant that The Double Door has provided thousands of nights of good entertainment for its neighbors," adds Margolin. "I [was] very at home on that bandstand. In a world that has gone to increasingly big-time corporate-marketed entertainment, the Double Door brings its bands and audiences together in a way that's real, in-the-moment, and ultimately more satisfying than watching TV, a computer, or seeing an elaborately staged arena show. The audience and the performers can meet and become friends. I know that running a live music club can be an opportunity to lose a lot of money and it's a tribute to Nick's strength and persistence that he [was] able to keep the place going."

"It was a job, but it was also 95 percent of my social life," Nick would later say. "The things I did enjoy was bringing these acts to Charlotte. Jo Dawkins brought in the Awareness Art Ensemble, which was the first reggae band to play Charlotte. I remember being at the bar in the afternoon, and I remember booking someone like the Nighthawks, and writing it down on a piece of paper, and just putting it on the board. And people would be like, The Nighthawks! Alright!" Just putting the poster up, it got everyone excited."

JAKE BERGER MAKES A POINT IN THE DRESSING ROOM, 1999. Photo by Daniel Coston

CALVIN "SANTA CLAUS" JACKSON AND NICK KARRES, FIFTH ANNIVERSERY PARTY, DECEMBER 1978.
Photo by Pat Shanklin/Double Door archives

STEVIE RAY VAUGHAN'S SIGNATURE, FOUND WEDGED BEHIND A MIRROR IN THE CLUB'S ORIGINAL RESTROOM. Photo by Daniel Coston

DOUBLE DOOR INN BAR, LATE 1970s.
Courtesy Double Door Inn archives

WORKERS REMOVE THE ORIGINAL WINDOW ON THE CLUB'S SECOND FLOOR, EARLY 1980s. Courtesy Double Door Inn archives

BOB MARGOLIN, LATE 1970s.
Courtesy Double Door Inn archives

CHAPTER TWO
Charlotte's Home Of The Blues
1980-2008

As the decade began, the Double Door Inn was as busy as ever, open seven days a week, throughout the year. No longer just a rowdy bar, or a place to eat and hang out, it had become a popular home for musicians that was lacking in Charlotte, and elsewhere. Be they locals that came in on Friday for Happy Hour, or national touring acts that desperately needed a place to play between Washington, DC and Atlanta, the Door was always open, and many poured through.

"In the early days, late 70s into the 80s, as I was getting my own music off the ground, seeing and hearing some of the great local and traveling bands that played at the Double Door was a huge part of my musical education," recalls longtime Charlotte musician Bill Noonan. "Then, playing there provided the opportunity both to improve as a musician and performer and to reach a bigger audience. That opportunity, as a local player just getting started, to improve and develop musical "credibility" is a huge part of the gift that Nick and the staff and audience at the Double Door gave to so many local musicians over the years."

"The Double Door was known among many musicians I knew as the place to play," remembered Bill Blue in 2008. Blue greatly admired the Nighthawks, and asked his agent to try and book him everywhere that the Nighthawks had played. "That was how I first came to play at the Double Door," he says. From the years from 1978 to 1984, Blue stated that the Double Door was considered one of the premier places for Blues musicians to play in the south. "I remember the very first time that my band played there. I was upstairs with my guys and I remember telling them that I wanted everyone to play really, really well. I definitely came of age in the music business during this time. We always had great gigs and Nick and

Matt always treated us very well each time we came to town. It was one of our all-time favorite places to play. One thing that really made this venue special was that people actually came out to listen to the music."

Another musician who that had found his way to the Door, as it was often referred to by this point, was an outrageous fellow known as Root Boy Slim. He was acquainted with the Nighthawks Band and that is one of the connections that landed him a spot on the calendar. His real name was Foster McKenzie III. His father was a golf course architect, and their family lived in Washington, DC.

McKenzie attended several prestigious private schools, and eventually ended up studying at Yale University, a bastion of the Ivy league. Root Boy, as he came to be known, made the acquaintance of a bass player named Bob Greenlee. Greenlee was also captain of the Yale football team, and a fraternity brother. The two kindred spirits formed a band known as Prince la-la Percy, Percy Uptight and the Midnight Creepers. Their most notable accomplishment was never playing the same venue twice.

Root Boy and Greenlee went on the road to play outrageous shows. Slim was a large man and he became known as "300 pounds of dynamite with a two-inch fuse." His band took on the name Root Boy Slim and the Sexchange Band. The band knew how to use shock lyrics and antics to draw the audience in. Slim often came on stage wearing a straitjacket and mumbled half-sentences and made often bizarre statements that made sense only to him. Slim passed away in Florida in 1993. To its final day, the Double Door had a framed poster that reads "Root Boy Slim & the Sexchange Band" mounted on the wall behind the bar.

Although they had played their first Double Door show the previous year, 1980 was the year that the Spongetones found their audience, and the crowds in turn found them. Jake Berger bowed out from the band after that first Double Door show, and Keith Brooks briefly joined the band. He was then replaced when Jamie Hoover joined the band in 1980.

"I remember playing in January or February of 1980," remembers Pat Walters. "There was a little snow and hardly anyone was there. We were all thinking, 'Well that was a nice experiment, time to get back to real life'. Jamie Hoover joined the band shortly after and we really gelled as a band after that. The crowds became

DOUBLE DOOR INN EXTERIOR, 1981.
Courtesy Double Door Inn archives

huge."

"I had seen the Spongetones a few times before I joined," says Jamie Hoover. "I did a session with Alan Kaufman at Bob Davis Studios, and Alan said, 'I want you to come over to the Double Door with me,' because he knew what was going down. The Spongetones were there, and the guy I replaced, Keith Brooks, was incredibly cool. He had gray hair, he had the right guitar strap, and I wanted that job worse than anything in the world.

"As soon as we got there, the band took a break, and we went over to where the front door was. And Pat was over there, being Pat, and he said, 'Hey, Keith wants to leave the band, and well, you're in.' And I was asked to join, right at the Double Door. And that was where we all first played together. Somewhere, I've got a recording of that first show where girls are screaming during 'Can't Buy Me Love.'" By 1982, their first album, Beat Music, was garnering rave reviews in Rolling Stone magazine, and bringing in some of the biggest crowds that the Double Door has ever seen.

"The crowds got big," recalls Steve Stoeckel. "At one point, we played incognito, with made-up names (Pud and the Whoppers, Rock Thrown Liberation Front, Jumpy and the Humors) mid week to have semi-secret gigs for Uber Fans."

"The Double Door was a dive, but it was a cool dive," adds Hoover. "The clean venues are the ones you gotta watch out for."

A Spongetones show also became the impetus for one of the venue's most recognizable features. When the locally-based TV show PM Magazine asked to do a story about a Spongetones show, Nick and Matthew Karres decided to show off the Double Door by painting the venue's logo on their back wall, which had been designed a few years before by Everette Carpenter. "Everette projected the logo on the back wall, and then he painted the logo, using the projection as a guide," says Nick. "Everette brought that logo in one day, and said that we could use it. I said, 'What do you want for it?' And he said, 'Just leave my name at the door, plus one.' So we did." Carpenter's name would remain at the door until his passing in 2013, and his logo stayed on the back wall until the day that the Double Door closed.

As the years went by, the two Karres brothers continued to work together doing

SPONGETONES POSTER, 1982.
Courtesy Double Door Inn archives

all of the work behind the scenes that must be attended to in order for a business to survive. They rotated shifts. Some evenings, Matthew would be on duty and Nick would work during the day. Depending on their own personal schedules, they rotated working hours so that both of them were able to keep the business going. "I went a long time without a day off," says Matthew Karres.

There was still some of the crowd that gave the Double Door its rough element. "It took us about ten years from when I started. That was a rough club," says Mandrapilias. "So much bad elements, as well as good. There were some tough times. Trying to promote all kinds of new stuff. But I loved it. When I started working there, Nick and Matt were ten years older than me, so for me, it was like I was working for the king. Everybody was covering everybody's back. Back then, in the late 70s and early 80s, this city rocked, and the Double Door was one of those places."

Occasionally, that hard work also came with some luck. Sometime around 1981, the old Chronosynclaticinfindibumum building burned, and was demolished in order to ease access to the small parking lot beside the Double Door.

"The Double Door Inn was my second home," says Mandrapilias. "I would tell people, 'We've got the best club in town. Come see this band. If you don't like them, I'll pay your cover charge.' And people would say, "I'll never doubt you again.' It gave me a place to anchor me. It was pretty damn awesome."

By 1982, the Double Door Inn was a busy place. When national acts weren't packing them in, local acts like the Spongetones, and the Federal Brothers were holding court. Stevie Ray Vaughan was playing the venue for his third and last time, before his management moved him into larger spaces. By this point, Nick Karres had heard a lot, and and seen a lot. One phone call would soon change the course of the Double Door's history.

"I received a phone call from an executive in New York who told me that we were going to have someone unexpected come into our business in about a month," remembers Nick Karres. "I had no idea who he was talking about. Later, I was driving home and I heard a radio ad for an upcoming Eric Clapton show at the "Chrome Dome" Coliseum. That was about the same time that we had the Legendary Blues Band scheduled for a show. Back then, that band consisted of

SPONGETONES, CD RELEASE PARTY FOR THEIR 11TH ALBUM, TOO CLEVER BY HALF, MAY 2008. Photo by Daniel Coston.

GEORGE MANDRAPILIAS TENDING BAR, EARLY 2008.
Photo by Daniel Coston

many former members of the Muddy Waters Band and they had played with Clapton previously. Jerry Portnoy was also in the band and when I heard the commercial, I felt chills go over my body.

"The Legendary Blues Band was scheduled for a Monday night show. We told a few people that they might want to drop by, but Clapton did not show. One of the most unusual things that happened was that we already had local musician Bill Noonan scheduled for that Thursday night, and Legendary Blues band had a scheduled gig in Atlanta. Their gig was cancelled, and they decided to spend a few days in Charlotte. This was one of the key events that made everything work." Clapton was basing his tour out of Charlotte at the same time. He, his managers and entourage were staying at the Radisson Hotel. Portnoy was talking to Clapton during this time and hoping to make something happen. Clapton played the Charlotte Coliseum on Wednesday night, June 23, but he did not come in that night. Many people still believe that this is the night he played at the Double Door after that show, but it did not happen that way. He actually came in on Thursday night, June 24, 1982, after playing a show in Tennessee and flying back to Charlotte. Clapton and Portnoy agreed that he would sit in with the Legendary Blues Band that night at the Double Door, in Charlotte. Then, Legendary Blues Band requested to play that night. In fact, Noonan still tells people that [he] got bumped for Clapton. We were never really certain if this appearance would really happen but we wanted to accommodate such a blues legend if at all possible."

"My band at the time, the Watchcats, were booked at the Double Door on a Thursday night," remembers Bill Noonan. "When we showed up to set up the PA and gear in the late afternoon, we saw on our poster that the Legendary Blues Band had been added to the bill. That was the band that had just played there the previous weekend, so we were a bit confused. Jo Dawkins, who booked the club at that time, swore me to secrecy and told me that Eric Clapton might show up to play with the Legendary Blues Band. You can understand that we took this news with a bit of skepticism. But, Jo put me in touch with Jerry Portnoy, the harp player in the Legendary Blues Band. The LBB, by the way, was three older black guys, including pianist Pinetop Perkins, who had been Muddy Waters' backup band, along with a couple of younger Jewish guys from the Northeast, playing traditional Chicago blues. So, I called Jerry Portnoy at the motel where they were staying. Jerry Portnoy could not have been more humble about the whole thing, and apologetic for crashing our gig. He explained that since Clapton, who had

ERIC CLAPTON WITH THE LEGENDARY BLUES BAND UPSTAIRS IN THE DRESSING ROOM, MARCH 1982. Jerry Portnoy, seated in center, directly behind Clapton, Pinetop Perkins seated next to Portnoy on his left.
Photo by Pat Shanklin/Courtesy Double Door Inn archives

played in Charlotte earlier that week, was still in the area, and this was an opportunity for him to play with the guys from Muddy Waters' old band. So I told him that if it actually came together, come on, and we'd accommodate.

"That night, we played a first set, then just about the time we were wrapping it up, I looked over to the door and there was Clapton and entourage coming up the steps. I turned to the band and said, 'One more song, guys'. We played one more tune, and turned it over to them. Jerry came up on the stage, introduced himself and Gary Brooker, the keyboardist from Clapton's band. Again, they could not have been more polite or appreciative. At that point, we did what we could to facilitate the happening. We got them plugged up. They used our PA and some of our other gear, brought in a couple of their own amps, a Wurlitzer electric piano on loan from Don Tillman at Tillman Music, and then we got out of the way. They got up and played old-school Chicago blues, and Clapton sat in with them in a very low key way, like he was just one of the guys in the band. Obviously for them, it was all about the music."

Clapton came into the Double Door sometime around midnight, and watched the band play for more than an hour. Karres estimates that there were about thirty-five people in attendance when Clapton arrived. Soon after he appeared, a long line at the pay phone in the front began to form, with patrons called friends and anyone else that they could reach. Clapton walked in with a number of people, including his road manager, and members of his band, which included Procol Harum singer and keyboardist Gary Brooker, and guitarist Chris Stainton.

Dillard Richardson, bass player with the Watchcats, also lent his gear to the Legendary Blues Band. "I had brought my camera with me, but Clapton's road manager didn't want any photos taken," Richardson later recalled. "He made me give my camera to Martino. Later that night, I got Martino to give me back my camera, and I snuck some photos of Clapton onstage. There was not a lot of light onstage that night." Richardson's photos are the only photos of Clapton playing at the Double Door, and Richardson would later use those photos as the basis for his painting of that night, which Nick Karres displayed in the club for many years.

By the time that Jerry Portnoy welcomed Clapton to the stage, there were maybe around ninety people actually present. Clapton plugged in a Stratocaster guitar and played five songs with the band, and then one encore, and did not sing.

ERIC CLAPTON, DOUBLE DOOR INN, JUNE 24, 1982
WITH THE LEGENDARY BLUES BAND.
All Photos by Dillard Richardson.

ERIC CLAPTON, DOUBLE DOOR INN, JUNE 24, 1982
WITH THE LEGENDARY BLUES BAND. Jerry Portnoy (harmonica), Pinetop Perkins (piano), Willie Smith (drums), Calvin "Fuzz" Jones (bass), Peter "HiFi" Ward (guitar).
All Photos by Dillard Richardson.

After the show, Clapton hung around with Portnoy and the band in their dressing room, by then known as the bar's green room. While there, local photographer Pat Shanklin orchestrated a posed photo of Clapton with the band, with Clapton lying on the floor, and this photo remains the best-known picture ever taken at the Double Door.

"Everyone that worked at the club went upstairs after the show to meet him," recalls Mandrapilias. "I didn't know what to say! He was very cool. He met everybody that worked there. It was beautiful, and one of the highlights of my life." For years after that show, whenever Clapton visited Charlotte, rumors would abound that he might once more stroll into the Double Door Inn again. In the intervening years, the people who "say" that they were there that night has grown well beyond those actual 60 to 90 people. The Double Door would later make a t-shirt for one of its anniversaries. The back of it read, "I was there when Eric played! Yeah, right!"

Around this time, Nick Karres had realized how important blues music was to his club, and what else he could do to support that music. The idea of becoming an affiliate of the International Blues Foundation by starting the Charlotte Blues society came from two sources. Three blues musicians, Beth Pollhammer, James Linton and Bill Buck, and Nick Karres. As the Double Door was the only club hiring blues musicians in the Charlotte area at the time, Karres had become interested in helping the Blues acts become more popular locally and boost interest in their music. During the first year of the founding of the Charlotte Blues Society, Beth Pollhamer worked with Nick and other society members to bring more people to their monthly meetings.

The society is affiliated with the International Blues Foundation located in Memphis, Tennessee. The purpose of the Foundation is to help preserve blues music. Each year, a contest is held in Memphis to determine who should be picked as the International Blues champion. There are two categories, band and solo/duo acts. Most of the Blues societies that are affiliates hold their own regional talent contests in order to pick who will represent them at the prestigious yearly contest. The Foundation also sponsors the Blues Music awards each year which is like the Grammy awards of the Blues. Many musicians who have won some of these awards (previously known as the Handy Awards), have played at the Double Door. In 1994, The Double Door was presented a special award for Keeping The Blues

MATTHEW AND NICK KARRES, DOUBLE DOOR INN 10TH
ANNIVERSARY SHOW, 1983. Courtesy Double Door Inn archives

PINETOP PERKINS, MAY 2004.
Photo by Daniel Coston

WILLIE DIXON'S CONTRACT FOR HIS APPEARANCE IN 1984.
Courtesy Double Door Inn archives

JUNIOR WALKER, 1984.
Courtesy Double Door Inn archives

Alive from the International Blues Foundation. In 2001, the IBC would recognize the Double Door Inn as the oldest blues venue in the United States operating under the same management, and oldest in the same location for this period of time. Only Antone's in Austin, Texas could lay claim to being older than the Double Door, although Antone's had changed names, and had been renovated. Despite this, Nick and the Charlotte Blues Society took pride in the Double Door definitively being the oldest blues music venue east of the Mississippi River.

"Back then, we were what was known as a "groundbreaker" club," says Nick Karres. "Being a groundbreaking club, we often hired bands that no one knew. That is, they were not always commercial successes and they weren't heard on the radio, but we took our chances. We sometimes really stuck our neck out, and sometimes we lost money. I feel that one of the best things we have done was to take many chances trying to do the right thing by providing great music. But we were definitely not driven by the bottom line. That is also part of the reputation and legacy of the Double Door. It has always been a risky venture. For example, the first time Stevie Ray Vaughan played here, we only had six people in the audience and that included the bartender. The second time he played here, we drew about thirty people and by the third and last time he played here, we had maybe about a hundred people turn out.

"Once you take so many chances over the years, it gives you a feeling I can't really describe. A serious businessperson would have never done business this way. If money had been my biggest motivator, I would have run a hotel bar and brought in top forty bands.

"I always have gotten my satisfaction from setting up great shows," adds Karres. "I don't have to be in the forefront of announcing from the stage. My satisfaction comes from making shows that feature great musicians possible. Unfortunately, it is hard to predict whether the business will make money on any one particular show. So it really has to be a labor of love to run a venue such as this one on such a small scale."

Many people in the Charlotte area have their own favorite Double Door story. There were couples who met and later married each other, as well as those who celebrated birthdays and anniversaries by treating themselves to a night out at the Double Door. The reputation of the business grew and more people decided to drop by to see what their friends were talking about.

"I would meet people," adds Rob Thorne, "and they would say, 'Oh, I've heard about the Double Door, but I'm not sure if I should go.' and I'd say, 'You've got to come. You've just got the experience the Double Door.' We've brought a lot of people that otherwise would've never gone there."

"The Double Door was the venue I could count on for legendary blues acts, but it was also more than that," says writer Jay Ahuja. "My wife and I met in a continuing education photography class at CPCC, so we walked up to the Double Door Inn for our first date. For years, we regularly discovered bands who were up-and-coming because Nick would give us a heads-up from time to time, saying, 'There's a band coming next week you should try to see.' There was never any pressure and he was always right about the quality of music. So, we got to see tremendous Blues, Zydeco and Americana musicians we already knew about and discover new music. To me, the Double Door Inn was a southern version of New York City's CBGB's. It was the club responsible for bringing countless bands to town that many of us would never have seen, if they didn't book them to play."

For many people in Charlotte, the Double Door Inn became the place for first dates, second dates, and more dates that led to marriage and children. "I was at Dan Hicks and the Hot Licks show in 1991 when I met my husband," says longtime patron Laura Fortson Elam. "We like to say that he slurred at me and I slurred back, and the rest is history."

"We were never a pick-up bar," adds Nick Karres. "People didn't come to the Double Door just for that, but a lot of people did meet at the Double Door, and later marry. I've heard a lot of those stories."

In 1984, Matthew Karres made the decision to move on from the bar business, and left to pursue other interests. "It was a lot of work. We never made as much money that people thought we did. On many nights, we didn't make enough to cover the band's guarantee at the door. So we had to take that out of our beer sales. You've got t-shirts you're giving away. That's all money out of your pocket. That being said, I met a lot of really great people. They've been the best friends I ever had, as well as having a lot of fun. I enjoyed the hell out of it."

As Matthew Karres left, new faces began to appear at the Double Door. One of those would become their door guy for 32 years, Todd Smith. "On my time working at the Double Door one would think that the best part would be hearing all of the great music that has been there throughout the years," says Smith. "Or meeting the musicians that played there or who just happened to venture in. Another would be meeting all the pro and amateur athletes that have come in. Whether football players, basketball, baseball, golf or NASCAR, they have all been in not to mention all of the local and national media that covered them. Meeting actors and actresses who played in movies that were shot at the DDI. Also politicians of all kinds have been through these doors. Also, there have been all sorts of opportunities that have come from working at the Double Door such as going to sporting events of all kinds, and I mean in first class, or getting to play golf at historic and exclusively private courses. or getting backstage passes to huge concerts due to dealing with booking agents. Or all the people I have met along the way, I have made a lot of friends that I hope I will have for the rest of my life."

"I can't say that all has been great, but for me it has always been about the laughs. When I was first hired, I also worked with Nick in the afternoons and met many of his childhood friends and heard all of their stories. I heard stories about Nick from high school, college and the early days of the Double Door Inn. If it's true that laughter adds years to one's life, then I should live a couple of hundred years. But the absolute best thing about working here is working for Nick Karres. Simply put, he is a good man who gives people chances. If it wasn't for Nick, there is no telling where we would all be today, and I want to thank him for that."

"By the 1980s, that scene of some of charlotte's first live music had given way to the blues era that gave the Double Door its claim to fame," Woody Mitchell would later recall. "Working in road bands most of that time, I stopped in every time I was in town and tried to keep up with folks. In 1992, I moved back to Charlotte for good and played there in numerous weekend warrior bands, including Woody & The Wingnuts, and the Stragglers, and staged or played numerous benefits along the way."

CLARENCE "GATEMOUTH" BROWN, 1984.
Courtesy Double Door Inn archives

JOHN HAMMOND, 1986.
Courtesy Double Door Inn archives

FABULOUS THUNDERBIRDS FLYER, 1985.
Courtesy Double Door Inn archives

DOUBLE DOOR INN FLYER, OCTOBER 1986.
Courtesy of Lenny Federal

DOUBLE DOOR INN 15TH ANNIVERSARY FLYER, 1988.
Courtesy Double Door Inn archives

DOUBLE DOOR INN 15TH ANNIVERSARY PARTY, DECEMBER 1988.
Courtesy Double Door Inn archives

Sponsoring benefits for musicians who were struck by some sort of physical illness or other tragedy has always been a custom at the Double Door. Over the years, countless benefits have been sponsored and held at the facility with all proceeds going to benefit musicians in need of medical care or other life necessities. Glancing at some of the old calendars, several benefits sponsored by the Double Door stand out. Benefits held for local musicians such as Bruce Schneider, Michael Federal and Charles Hairston are just a few of the names that leaped off the page. It is well known throughout Charlotte's music community that if space is needed to stage a show to help raise money for anyone in need, Nick Karres always went out of his way to help in any way possible.

Over the years, there have been many stories of the generosity that is a large part of Nick's outlook on life. In order to prevent any embarrassment no names will be used but it is well-known that many bad checks have remained uncollected, loans have not been repaid and many outright gifts have been given to some of the less fortunate by both Karres brothers. During an interview conducted with Nick, he expressed his feelings vehemently about such matters. "It has always been important to me personally to try and always do the right thing."

The Double Door continued to bring in a variety of acts throughout the 1980s. A walk through the club and looking through the photos on the wall revealed the variety of people that played there. Buddy Guy, Vassar Clements, Jason And The Scorchers, Roy Buchanan, Steve Forbert, Sugar Blue, Wanda Jackson, John Hammond, Clarence "Gatemouth" Brown, Wet Willie, Steve Earle and many others graced the stage, while local acts such as the Federal Bureau Of Rock & Roll held down regular Sunday or Monday shows.

Another local band that attracted a lot of attention throughout the 1980s and '90s was the Belmont Playboys, a punk-rockabilly band that brought a different crowd to the Double Door. "A Belmont Playboys show was a full-on event for a lot of people," continues Coston. "Their crowd was predominantly filled with rockabilly fans, who would drink at the front of the stage, and dance behind the soundboard. some of the best photos I have ever taken of dancers were at Belmont Playboys shows."

Any business entity depends on many professional and personal relationships in order to keep things running as smoothly as possible. The Double Door was no

CAREY BELL, 2005.
Photo by Daniel Coston

MOOKIE BRILL WITH NAPPY BROWN, DECEMBER 2006.
Photo by Daniel Coston

ROY BUCHANAN, 1988. BUCHANAN DIED A WEEK AFTER THIS SHOW.
Courtesy Double Door Inn archives

GLENN PHILLIPS BAND, 1985.
Photo by Rackley/Double Door archives

exception. It would be impossible to name all of the people who contributed to the venue's longevity. One class of people that have played a large part in the story over the years are the booking agents, who assist in getting bands "booked" into venues like the Double Door.

Even though Charlotte is certainly not considered an entertainment base, three of the most successful blues booking agents in the country are located in Charlotte. Piedmont Talent, Blue Mountain and Intrepid Artists grew out of a scene that the Double Door helped to support. If you could play the Double Door Inn, you could play anywhere.

Rick Booth founded his own agency, Intrepid Artists, in 1994. "I used to sneak in with a fake ID back in the early 80s to see the Spongetones and Cruis-O-Matic. I was not there to drink, only to see the music. I knew that if I went down there, I would be in for a treat. Back then, you only had to be eighteen to frequent clubs or drink. We all had fake ID's. I assume that things became more difficult when the drinking age changed to twenty-one. It was all harmless good fun."

At that time, Booth had no idea that one day he would be a booking agent and do business with the Double Door. "Some of the first bands that I booked there were Jimmy Thackery & the Assassins, followed by Jimmy Thackery & the Drivers, Johnny "Clyde" Copeland, Chubby Carrier and the Bayou Swamp Band. Over the years, I have booked the likes of Son Seals, Walter Trout, Tab Benoit, Tinsley Ellis, Watermelon Slim, Lil' Ed & the Blues Imperials and many, many more.

"[Nick] is one of a kind!" adds Booth. "There are a lot of people in this world that could learn some diplomacy and many other lessons from Nick."

It should be noted that the Double Door Inn stands for different things to different people. Many people frequent the bar for a quick bite of lunch or a drink between classes at CPCC. Many of these customers may never see a live music show at the venue, yet these folks are also part of the history.

"I didn't really come to know the Double Door Inn as most people have," says writer Lynn Farris. "True, I've spent plenty of nights at the club partying with friends, checking out bands, but the first time I walked into the place it was early afternoon, after classes at Central Piedmont Community College across the

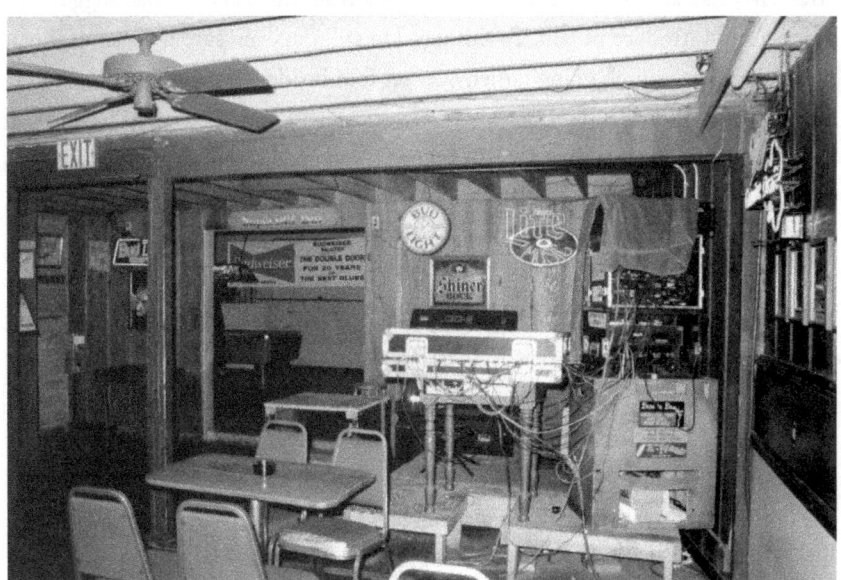

SOUND BOARD AND BACK ROOM, 1993.
Courtesy Double Door Inn archives

LENNY FEDERAL MANNING THE SOUNDBOARD, MID 1990s.
Courtesy Double Door Inn archives

street. My dad and my brother, friends of Nick from the ball field, had suggested I stop by and introduce myself. To this day, I'm still not even sure if either of them, particularly my church going father, ever set foot inside the club.

"Being only eighteen at the time, the hours I'd accrued patronizing nightclubs was limited, but taking a seat at the Double Door's bar for lunch that day, I looked around and knew I was in a cool place. From the start, I was treated like family, and soon I was spending a lot of time at the Double Door, which may very well be the reason I spent five years at a two year college. But putting in your time during the day offered a different perspective. I had my own breakfast special and Nick even cut me a deal on parking after my car was vandalized at a regular CPCC parking lot. Late afternoons, I'd stop in to hang out with the happy hour regulars because everybody always had a story to tell. Back then, Nick's wife Betty worked the lunch counter with one of his longtime buddies, Basil. Todd, who a lot of folks now know from working the door at night, was the cook. Missy [who worked at the Double Door throughout the 1990s] came in during the afternoons to help with the bookings and also helped longtime bartenders Mike and George when they needed it. and every once in awhile I'd see Kelly or Cole, Nick and Betty's kids. The Double Door Inn played a significant part of my life."

Throughout the 1980s, and in the early 1990s, Nick Karres started making changes to the Double Door. He removed the booths in the main room. The bar was extended. In 1982, he removed the display window on the building's second floor, which was left over from the Peggy Houston Lamp Shop days. In the early 1990s, he added the bathrooms at the end of the game room, and walled off the venue's original bathrooms. One fix that he hadn't planned on making, however was when Hurricane Hugo blew through Charlotte on September 22nd of 1989.

"I don't remember much about the night that Hugo hit," says Nick Karres. "The night before, the Nighthawks had played, and I had stayed up late, hanging out with them. The Truly Dangerous Swamp Band played the night that Hugo hit, and were done by the time that it hit, but I was trying to sleep that night, after having been up with the Nighthawks the night before.

"We had some damage, the next day. The windows in my office and green room had been pushed in, and papers were blown all over the room. A little exterior damage, but it wasn't too bad."

FRIENDS AND BAR HELP OF THE DOUBLE DOOR INN, EARLY 1990s.
Courtesy Double Door Inn archives

BASIL TAKES CARE OF PATRONS, MID 1990s.
Courtesy Double Door Inn archives

The decade from 1990 to 2000 were years that were mostly good ones, as far as the venue was concerned. It was a time when local and regional bands played regularly and some of the national traveling acts were often booked and played to good crowds. Part Time Blues Band, Big Brick Building, Tab Benoit, Bob Margolin, Bernard Allison, Tinsley Ellis, Kenny Neal, Smokin' Joe Kubek, and Luther Allison also made appearances as well as others too numerous to recount. In 1993, the Double Door Inn celebrated its twentieth anniversary with a show at the Capri Theater. Jimmy Thackery, Tinsley Ellis, and Don Dixon & Marti Jones headlined a show that also saw Nick take the stage to thank the audience for their support, which received a rousing ovation.

Throughout the 1990s, the Double Door continued to acquire more staff. Missy McCall was a fixture at the venue for several years, and specialized in a laugh that could be heard over the loudest of bands. Kevin Outlaw, another longtime doorman, began working for Karres in March of 1997. His employment began in an informal way. By the time he was twenty-one, he began to hang out as a customer and became known to the night bartenders, Mike and George. At some point, there was a need for someone to fill in at the crucial post of doorman and when asked, Outlaw enthusiastically agreed. Later, the job became six nights a week for a while, but then as he found daytime employment, he became a part-time employee again.

Being the first person that a potential customer encounters as they enter the building for a music event, "Evaluating people as they come in and being able to screen out potential troublemakers [was] my most important function", says Outlaw. "Initially, I wanted to work here regardless of whether I was paid. I've just always thought that this was such a cool place."

One anecdote Outlaw shares goes a long way towards explaining why he finds the venue so appealing. "Before I started working here, I just happened to be here one afternoon. I observed something that really made me realize the significance of a business like this. There was a CEO of a major corporation, dressed in a professional suit, having a beer at the bar. Beside him was a man who drove a garbage truck for a living. In here, over a beer, the two were having a great conversation. Outside of here, the two would have never spoken a word to each other. That image has stayed with me to this day."

DON DIXON AND MARTI JONES BACKSTAGE AT THE DOUBLE DOOR INN'S 20 ANNIVERSARY SHOW, CAPRI THEATER, DECEMBER 1993.
Courtesy Double Door Inn archives

BERNARD ALLISON PLAYING ON TOP OF THE DOUBLE DOOR BAR, 1997.
Courtesy Double Door Inn archives

TODD SMITH THE DOORMAN, JULY 2008.
Photo by Daniel Coston

DOORMAN KEVIN OUTLAW, JUNE 2008.
Photo by Daniel Coston

THE DOUBLE DOOR, 1990s.
Courtesy Double Door Inn archives

GREGG MCGRAW, AMERICANA NIGHT PROMOTER WITH NICK KARRES,
1997. Courtesy Double Door Inn archives

LEON RUSSELL, MAY 1998.
Photo by Daniel Coston

RANK OUTSIDERS, AMERICANA NIGHT'S CELEBRATION OF
THE DOUBLE DOOR INN'S 25TH ANNIVERSERY, DECEMBER 1998.
Photo by Daniel Coston

MONDAY NIGHT ALL-STARS, FALL 1998.
Photo by Daniel Coston

LES MOORE HELPS NICK TO PLAY GUITAR, LATE 1990s.
Courtesy Double Door Inn archives

LOU FORD, 1998.
Photo by Daniel Coston

TIFT MERRITT, JUNE 1998.
Photo by Daniel Coston

"I remember the night that Tom Jones came in," recalls George Mandrapilias. "Someone said, 'What are you going to do?' And I said, 'I'm going to thank you for coming into my club.' And I did. People would come from Germany to see the club, and then come back years later, and say, 'Wow! You're still here!" By 1997, there was an emerging scene of musicians throughout North Carolina that infused rock with country and folk music, a mix that was often tagged with the "Americana" label. The Double Door quickly became home to a collective of americana acts like the rank outsiders, and David Childers. Gregg McCraw, who had been promoting Rank Outsiders shows, also began promoting an "Americana Night" series every Tuesday evening, bringing in national acts to play alongside the local groups.

"The showcase itself evolved during its five-year life," remembers Gregg McCraw. "During the first year, we started to bring in local guest artists. That evolved to regional artists, and then national touring artists. The first was Mary Cutrufello." "Gregg McCraw's Americana series was just fantastic," recalls photographer Daniel Coston. "I saw so many people that I still listen to through that Tuesday night showcase, many of whom I would have never seen. Six String Drag, Mercury Dime, Freakwater, Steve Wynn with the Continental Drifters, Mark Olson and Victoria Williams. Deke Dickerson, a photo of which later became the cover of his best-of CD. Alejandro Escovedo's performance in April of 1998 is still one of the best shows I have ever seen in my life. Two guitars, a cello and a violin sounding like an orchestra. As a photographer, you know that you're on to something when you only intend to shoot one roll of film, and proceed to shoot all the film in your bag."

"There were some tremendous shows during those five years," adds McCraw. "The 'Known On The Underground' CD release party. The Drive-By Truckers and Slobberbone on stage together, and the Slobberbone bassplayer hanging from the rafters over the stage. Robbie Fulks' energetic destruction of a mic stand during a Michael Jackson cover. Dave Alvin pounding his semi-functional amp during a marathon evening until his rings cut his fingers open, and he left the stage bleeding. That was the same night Todd [Smith] tossed a drunk out the door, and across the hood of my car."

Along with the Americana scene, there was a new scene of bands that were bringing in crowds to the Double Door. Popular locals acts such as Lou Ford, and

LINK WRAY, 1998.
Photo by Daniel Coston

ALEJANDRO ESCOVEDO, MAY 1998.
Photo by Daniel Coston

DAVE ALVIN, DECEMBER 1999.
Photo by Daniel Coston

R. L. BURNSIDE.
Photo by Daniel Coston

DRIVE BY TRUCKERS, SOUTHERN ROCK OPERA TOUR, 2001.
Photo by Daniel Coston

Electro-luxe (later renamed Come On Thunderchild) filled up the Double Door's calendar, along with shows from the likes of Ronnie Dawson, R. L. Burnside, Leon Russell, Buddy Miles, Levon Helm, and Link Wray, who played two shows at the bar in 1998.

"Link Wray was such a cool guy, and really nice to his fans," remembers Coston. "When he came back the second time, I made my way upstairs and gave him my photos from his first Double Door show. Link profusely thanked me for the photos, and told me how great a photographer I was. It really shook my system to have him be so complimentary."

One group that would become Charlotte's most popular artists were not even noticed, or even considered Charlotteans for their first years together. Brothers Scott and Seth Avett grew up in the Concord area, and had played around town in bands such as Margo, and the thrash-punk outfit Nemo. By 2001, the brothers had begun playing as Nemo: The Back Porch Project. Later that year, the group had become a trio with the addition of bassist Bob Crawford, who had played The Double Door Inn as part of Old 454, and the Memphis Quick 50. They had also settled on the name of The Avett Brothers.

While the Brothers played other venues, such as Fat City, and The Wine Vault many more times, it was the Double Door Inn where the trio recorded their first-ever live album on April 17th of 2002. The show was held on a Wendesday night, on a double bill with another local group, the Eric Lovell Band. The show was recorded direct to CD through the soundboard, and it is soundman Les Moore's voice that introduces the band, and the album. In retrospect, the album is a snapshot of a group still on the rise, mixing covers with some of their earliest original songs. It would also be the first full-length album that many Avett fans would hear.

"In January of 2003, David Childers asked a band he had just met, the Avett Brothers to open for him at the Double Door," adds Coston. "The Avetts had played the Double Door a few times before that, but was the first time that many of David's fans had seen or heard of them. Even then, their shows had a lot of energy, and you could just tell that they had something different. A lot of people came to see David that night, but they left talking about the Avetts."

SETH AVETT, JANUARY 2003.
Photo by Daniel Coston

DAVID CHILDERS, 2000.
Photo by Daniel Coston

LES MOORE, 1999.
Photo by Daniel Coston

BUDDY MILES, MAY 1999.
Photo by Daniel Coston

LEVON HELM & THE BARN BURNERS, JANUARY 2000.
Photo by Daniel Coston

One person that helped redefine the sound of the Double Door during these years was Les Moore. According to Rob Thorne, "I first saw Les Moore in the early '70s. Back then, Festival in The Park wouldn't let pop or rock musicians play the main stage. So Melvin [Cohen], who ran Reliable Music, set up his own side stage for people to play, and he brought Les Moore in. Les was doing songs off of his Capricorn Records album, and he was just incredible. Years later, I met him when he started running sound at the Double Door, and I said that something seemed familiar about him. I finally realized that he was the guy I'd seen at Festival in the Park."

"I call New Orleans home, but I came to Charlotte by way of Austin, Texas where my wife attended school," said Moore in 2008. "I had played in New Orleans when I was off from my regular job on a towboat. Eventually, we moved to Charlotte when my wife landed a job here. I didn't really play until we had been here for about eight or nine years. I first started playing at Lenny Federal's open mic night at a place called Ty's. There I met Bobby Donaldson, who helped me get a job playing at the Sunset Lounge. While playing there, I met Jim Brock, Daryle Rice and many other local musicians. So I started thinking that I had accumulated all kinds of equipment over the years so I decided to just load it up and bring it along one night just to see what would happen. We started to attract all sorts of musicians who just wanted to play and my open stage evolved from that. I worked at several more venues but eventually, I had a chance to go to work at the Double Door. Nick told me that it didn't matter how many people came out. He wanted to provide the venue and even told me that he would help me unload my truck! It was all about the music for Nick."

Les ran the soundboard and set up the stage for many musicians during his time at the Double Door. For years after he left Charlotte, many musicians that returned to the Double Door would ask how Les was doing. In addition, the bar's famed Monday Night All-stars came together with his guidance. According to Moore, the original band on Monday night consisted of Jim Brock on drums, Bobby Donaldson on guitar, Rick Blackwell on bass, Johnny Alexander on horns, and Moore on guitar.

The original vocalist for the band, Charles Hairston, had been in different bands for most of his adult life. Hairston was the ultimate showman. Once he hit the stage, all eyes followed him as he sang, roared, strutted, and danced until he was

MUDDY WATERS BAND VETERANS MAC ARNOLD (ON LEFT) AND WILLIE SMITH, JUNE 2006.
Photo by Daniel Coston

(Left to Right) HUBERT SUMLIN, WILLIE SMITH, CAREY BELL, BOB MARGOLIN, MAY 2006. Photo by Daniel Coston

perspiring heavily. Percussionist Jim Brock had toured with several major musicians, as had Rick Blackwell. Johnny Alexander had played horns of all makes and models since childhood. The flute, soprano sax, alto sax, as well as the baritone sax, and would often play two saxophones at the same time in harmony.

Over the years, the Double Door also turned up in a few movies, most notably in Shallow Hal in 2001. "I knew that they were in town," says Nick, "and someone had called me and said, "This might happen'. They needed a roadhouse for a scene. Since it was a big movie studio, the bigwigs would come by and check the place out. One day, a bus showed up, and about eight or ten people walked in, checked out the place, and then walked out. Later on they called, and we signed a contract.

"Movies sets are big productions. People wait all day to do their one job. The Farrelly brothers were nice, and one of them in particular was very nice. I could have been best friends with Jack Black. I had a lot of fun talking to him. And it was cool to see the place on film. We were also used in two other TV movies. No Recourse, which starred Rachel Ward, and the TV mini-series called Shake, Rattle & Roll."

After the attack on the World Trade center in September of 2001, many businesses saw a downturn including the Double Door. During the early part of the twenty-first century, Karres was able to keep the business going, finding different ways to make sure that the bills were always paid.

"If I won money from a lottery ticket, it would go back into the bar", says Nick. "I had season tickets to the Panthers, and the first time that they went to the Super Bowl, I won two tickets to the Super Bowl, and I ended up selling them to a ticket broker. But that money didn't go into my pocket, it went to 1218 Charlottetowne Avenue."

Despite that, the Double Door still had plenty to celebrate. One of the most exciting things that the Charlotte Blues Society accomplished was sending a band to the national competition that actually won the IBC. Jim Jervis, a former member of the society shared the story with me. "I received an unsolicited CD by a band out of Atlanta called Delta Moon, from their manager, Nancy Lewis Pegel with Brilliant Productions. She was looking to try and get a local gig for the band. I had received plenty of CDs from bands as the vice president of the Blues Society.

I remember it clearly. I was headed out of town on vacation and just happened to bring along the Delta Moon CD. I was struck by the grizzly, mud-drenched sound coming out. I mean, that I was just blown away, and I said to my wife, 'You have to hear these guys. They have it!' Gina Leigh's and Tom Gray's vocals intertwined with Mark [Johnson] and Tom's dual slide guitars backed by a powerful rhythm section just grabbed me!

"I called Nancy and told her that I loved this band. This was a first for me. I quickly was able to make a couple of calls and I got them a gig at the Sylvia Theater in York, SC. I had to see them live. They played to about fifteen people. The lack of a crowd did not affect them at all. I began to think about our talent contest. I played the CD for a few folks, most of which loved it. I did have another board member that said to me that he didn't think they stood a chance against some of the other people who were going to compete. I told him otherwise and I said, 'I have your winner here.'"

"The group was reluctant," adds Jervis. "I definitely had to push. I told them that based on my knowledge of the other bands competing I felt that they had as good a chance as anyone to win the CBS contest and go on to Memphis and win it all. The competition was stiff that year, as it always is. We have a very strong base of fantastic musicians in this area. I had also negotiated a first place prize of 1,000 CDs and some free studio time for the winner. This helped get the band onboard. I also stressed to them that it would help them get a booking at the Double Door which they had not been able to crack before. It did help. They won our Contest in Charlotte in 2002, and went on to win in Memphis in early 2003."

Another artist that emerged at the Double Door during this time was Robin Rogers. After moving to Charlotte in 1990, she began to get involved with the Charlotte Blues Society. After marrying guitarist Tony Rogers, the two began performing as a duo. It was another Double Door mainstay, Jim Brock that encouraged the two to record their first CD, Time For Myself, in 2001.

By 2003, Robin and Tony had put together a band, and won the 2003 Charlotte Blues Society's Blues Challenge. While Robin did not win the national competition a few months later, Robin emerged as one of the nine finalists, and fans and fellow musicians began to take note. She would go on to record three more albums, and receive international acclaim for her singing, songwriting and powerful story.

The Double Door Inn also stayed involved with the music community through benefits, as it had done for years. Benefits for Charles Hairston, Robin Rogers, Jake Berger, Mike Martin, David Floyd and others would provide many special nights at the Double Door during its last fifteen years.

"We held a benefit for David Floyd, who played with a number of people in town," recalls Nick Karres. "Arthur Smith came by and performed a few numbers. Maurice Williams came by and performed a couple of songs, as well. He performed "Stay". I thought that was so cool. Performing that song, at our place."

Even if audiences were not as consistently large as they had once been, the venue could still provide a great show that one would never forget. "One of the best times I ever had at the Double Door was when Hubert Sumlin came to play in 2006, says Daniel Coston. "Hubert was the guitarist for Howlin' Wolf for 24 years, and redefined what a guitar player could do with both Blues and Rock music. Hubert was also one of the oldest children I have ever met in my life, in that he lived life with this childlike wonder. I wish more people in this world had that sense of excitement that he had. And he was always dressed in a very fine suit. "Hubert's band for the evening included Bob Margolin, and Willie Smith. Both had played with Muddy Waters at different times, as had Sumlin. Smith had also played with Clapton at the Double Door Inn in 1982, as part of the Legendary Blues Band. As the show began, former Muddy Waters harmonica player Carey Bell walked in and sat down next to the stage. Carey was living at that time with Mookie Brill, who accompanied Carey to the gig.

"From the start, everyone wanted to get Carey up on stage to join the band. Everyone except Carey, who sat there and shook his head anytime somebody asked. Mookie got up on stage and played, and Carey didn't move. Hubert even introduced Carey onstage at one point, and Carey just waved Hubert off.

This went on to two sets, albeit two killer sets of music. Somewhere around 1:30am, as the band got ready to play their final numbers, Bob Margolin looks down at Carey and says, 'Are you playing, man?' Carey shook his head, no. Bob said, 'Okay,' and starts to turn away, at which point Carey held up his index finger, indicating that he would do one song. Carey had been waiting all night to keep people guessing, and waiting to become the focus of attention. As Margolin quickly began to introduce Carey, Hubert stood onstage and began yelling, 'Yeah!

Yeah!' like an excited Little Leaguer. Carey proceeded to play three Muddy Waters songs with the band, four Muddy vets onstage together tearing it up. Real freaking history, live on stage at the Double Door."

Another favorite show of Coston's was Pinetop Perkins' return to the Double Door in 2004. "Pinetop Perkins was also part of the Legendary Blues Band, and another legend that I put up there with Hubert Sumlin. I remember arriving early for his show, only to find him sitting up against the wall, chatting with fans. Pinetop was so used to fans coming up and wanting to have their photos taken with him, that he couldn't figure out why I was just taking photos of him, and not of Pinetop with other folks around the bar.

"The Pinetop show was also the first time that I saw the legendary Nappy Brown. He came onstage during the middle of the show, and proceeded to roll all over the stage, began to undress while sitting on a woman's lap, and generally took over the building for his twenty-minute slot. There were so many shows that I'm so glad I saw during that time. Brian Auger, Sean Costello, Peter Tork, Robin Rogers. The list is endless."

In 2006, Don Dixon booked a Thursday night show at the venue. Dixon truly is one of the founding fathers of modern music in North Carolina, having led Arrogance for many years, and then going on to produce acts as varied as REM, Hootie & The Blowfish, and many others. Don also played the venue's 20th anniversary show with his wife and musical counterpart, Marti Jones, so this show was a welcome return for those who had followed his music.

Don's band for the evening included half of Hootie & The Blowfish. As the show progressed, the rest of Hootie, including singer Darius Rucker, took the stage, and Dixon yielded to the band playing a surprise eight-song set, in the smallest venue that the band had played in some time. There wasn't a long line at the Double Door's lone pay phone, as there was when Clapton showed up. Many happy fans quickly grabbed their cell-phones, taking photos, and telling their friends about what they were missing.

There's the night in 2001 that Al Kooper showed up to play with the Monday Night All stars. Dallas Mavericks owner Mark Cuban showed up at the venue with star center Dirk Nowitzki in tow, and both enjoyed the Allstars' set, and posed for photos with fans. AC/DC guitarist Angus Young often visited the Double Door while on tour, often enjoying the music while being largely unrecognized.

In November of 2007, Micah Davidson was hired at first to work in the kitchen. Several months before, Davidson had formed an organization dedicated to staging live music shows, the Carolinas Live Music Society. His knowledge of the music business was soon put to use, and he began to assist Nick in booking bands for the venue. Many of the older blues acts were no longer touring, but there is an amazing amount of live music available.

"The style may be a little different from the conventional blues music that made us famous, but many of the blues stars do not tour as much as they once did," said Mike Martin during that time. "Those who do still tour, often must have financial guarantees to appear at all. That means that we have no choice but to charge at the door. That is a difficult concept for some of our younger customers to accept." Bringing in Micah Davidson to help with the booking duties is a decision that Martin sees as an inevitable part of the change needed to sustain the venue into the 21st century. "Over the past few months, I have heard some really killer bands that Micah has booked."

When asked in 2008, Nick Karres said, "One of the biggest things that I am proud of is what we've accomplished. Not that this has been a huge business success, but I've always believed in doing the best you can with what you have. This facility was not built for music. It was originally someone's home. But as we got into presenting live music shows, we became a groundbreaking club. I wish I had all of the money that we have lost on bands but we put our money where it counted, by taking chances on bands, having both good nights as well as bad ones. The thing that I am most proud of is just how much we did accomplish. We took the chances, we rolled the dice all the time. I would hope that we have provided good music and good memories for our patrons over the years."

The Double Door Inn celebrated its 35th anniversary with a mixture of celebration and heavy hearts. When Monday Night Allstars leader Charles Hairston fell ill, a benefit was held that September to help raise money for his treatment. The show was definitely a night that reminded everyone of just how fragile a life can be, with longtime fans packing the venue. The many musicians who turned out in support of this cause showed the best side of the Charlotte live music community.

BETTYE LAVETTE, 2006.
Photo by Daniel Coston

MICAH IN HIS OFFICE, AUGUST 2008.
Photo by Daniel Coston

TRACIE LEWIS WORKING BEHIND THE BAR, AUGUST 2008.
Photo by Daniel Coston

TRACY ABERNETHY (ON RIGHT) AND TODD SMITH PREPARE FOR THE EVENING'S PATRONS, JULY 2008. Photo by Daniel Coston

BEN JOPLIN, LONGTIME MAINTENENCE MAN FOR THE DOUBLE DOOR INN.
Photo by Daniel Coston

KARRES FAMILY, 35TH YEAR DOUBLE DOOR BOOK-CLOSING PARTY,
JUNE 8, 2008. Photo by Daniel Coston

The year closed with the venue's 35th anniversary show, and the debut of Home Of The Blues, a book about the venue's history to date.

At the end of Home Of The Blues, Kelly Karres, daughter of Nick, was asked to talk about her thoughts and memories of the Double Door Inn, a building that she had known for literally for entire life.

"Because Nick is my father, I have a unique perspective of the Double Door. I remember walking into The Double Door with my father on Saturday mornings, with Wad's OrangeAde in my tiny hands. I can still hear the old hardwoods creaking beneath my feet as we walked into the building. Even as a little girl, I sensed a distinct connection to things past in that old building. Things not only existed, but still exist. With its dark shadows, long staircases and tall ceilings, the house invited my curiosity. As I stood still, The old walls seemed to talk to me, telling me a story.

"As a young girl this experience made me feel very special, as if someone was telling me a secret I wasn't supposed to hear. Now that I am older, I understand that these voices in the walls belong to many different people. They are the voices of the family that once called this building home. They are the voices of every musician, Patron and worker. They are the voices of every person who has entered the building and, in some way, has been touched by it.

"The next time that you walk into the Double Door, stay quiet and listen to the hardwoods creak beneath your feet. You, too, may just be lucky enough to hear those old walls talk."

NICK KARRES AT THE 35TH YEAR DOUBLE DOOR BOOK-CLOSING PARTY, JUNE 8, 2008. Photo by Daniel Coston

THE FAMOUS BELL AND HORN BEHIND THE BAR, SOUNDED OFF
WHENEVER SOMEONE TIPPED THE BARTENDER.
Photo by Daniel Coston

CHAPTER THREE

I'm Gonna Miss It

2009-2017

As the Double Door approached its 35th anniversary, the neighborhood surrounding the Double Door Inn had already begun to change rapidly. Longtime staples of the Elizabeth/Charlottetowne corridor were fading fast. Anderson's restaurant had just closed. The Athens restaurant, which had often been the scene of many show "after-parties", was about to be demolished, and Jimmie's Restaurant had already been turned into rubble. Central Piedmont Community College was taking up more and more of the neighborhood. Even the street that the Double Door occupied had been changed to Charlottetowne Avenue, to avoid confusion with the other end of Independence Boulevard that now reached into the next county.

Several months after Charles Hairston's benefit show, he passed away in February 2009, after months of battling cancer. Robin Rogers also fell ill during this time. Again, the Double Door Inn audiences stepped up with love, support, and benefit shows. When Rogers passed away from cancer in December of 2010, her story had been chronicled by NPR, and a wealth of fans around the world.

Through all of this, the Double Door continued on into its fifth decade. Where Charles Hairston once dazzled every Monday night, Shana Blake had taken his place with the Allstars. Bill Hanna played to jazz fans new and old every Tuesday night. The old groups many have changed band members, or broken up, but new bands came to take their place. Lou Ford fans would come to see the Loudermilks, while the Rank Outsiders faithful would go see Gigi Dover & The Big Love, and the Loose Lugnuts.

"My first Double Door Inn performance was opening for Gigi Dover And The Big Love," remembers Kevin Marshall, a Charlotte-based musician and guitar luthier.

"I was terrified that night. That stage was very intimidating. After that, It became home. Unfortunately, I did not get to play there enough times but the dozen or so times I did were always very inspirational. The musical spirits in that room are huge. I could play there and the next morning I would be up writing a song. To say you played there at all is big."

In 2011, Micah Davidson left the Double Door in pursuit of other opportunities. In his place came a familiar face. By 2012, Gregg McCraw had become one of the biggest show promoters in the area, bringing many acts to Charlotte in multiple venues across town. McCraw began to host established and new acts, reestablishing the reputation that the Double Door had early on as a "turnkey" venue. Legends such as Billy Joe Shaver, Ray Wylie Hubbard, Pete Anderson, and Bill Kirchen. Those acts also included Leogun, who played the venue in the summer of 2013 before heading out to open a nationwide tour for Kiss. Other young bands come to the Double Door to play where Clapton and Stevie Ray Vaughan played, and where the Avett Brothers played some of their earliest shows.

"We played the Double Door for the first time in 2012 when we released a record called, Come On In," says Sam Tayloe, of the Charlotte-based band, Time Sawyer. "I don't remember if it was a good show or not, but I do remember all the framed photos on the wall. That was my first taste of starting to get the picture, but really seeing the whole picture would take me a while. All I really knew of the Double Door at that time was from a bootleg I had from The Avett Brothers first live recording. Once music consumed my life, I was able to really understand the magnitude of that place. Everyone talks about Clapton, SRV, Buddy Guy, all the blues greats playing there, but what that really means is these guys wanted to come to the Double Door. Chose the Double Door. The Double Door was a place that passed the test. Over and over."

Another notable show during 2013 was when Pegi Young, then-wife of Neil Young, played the Double Door on a Tuesday night. Pegi's band was made up of musicians that had also collaborated with her husband. This included Rick Rosas, who joined Neil for a Buffalo Springfield reunion in 2010 and 2011, and the legendary keyboardist and songwriter Spooner Oldham. Walking into the Double Door, and seeing Oldham sitting right in front of you reminded many of how special the venue truly was.

PEGI YOUNG, 2013.
Photo by Daniel Coston

LEOGUN, 2013.
Photo by Daniel Coston

Around this time, the forty years of running the Double Door non-stop began to catch up with Nick. "I got really sick. I was in the hosptial for two months. I nearly died. And I knew that contributing to that was running the club for forty years. I was burned out."

But Karres returned, and kept going. And continued to give back to those that worked with him. When Mike Martin fell ill later that year, Karres organized a benefit concert to help pay Martin's medical bills. A packed house turned the benefit into a raucous party, with a camera rigged up so that Martin would watch all of the festivities from his hospital bed.

The next few years brought continued change to the neighborhood surrounding the Double Door. The trolley lines that had once passed the Wearn estate were brought back. New businesses began to pop up in front of Presbyterian Hospital. Despite increased traffic in the Elizabeth corridor, a new wave of growth was taking hold in Charlotte, and local music venues began to close. Despite that, the Double Door celebrated its 42th anniversary in December of 2015 with another packed show by the Federal Bureau Of Rock & Roll. For many, the venue had been there their entire adult lives. It had survived when so many others had faded away. It would always be there, many had thought. Very few there that night had any idea what the next year would bring.

"When I heard that David Kavah was in trouble, I knew that it would be bad for us," says Nick Karres. David Kavah had owned the property alongside the Double Door for many years. Kavah and Karres had gotten along, even so far on joining up to get their properties rezoned in the early 1990s, which allowed Nick to do work on the back of the venue.

"The first thing I heard [in 2015] was that he was in bankruptcy, and in foreclosure," adds Nick. "And my first thought was, that means he's gonna have to sell. He tried to get out of it, but he couldn't get anyone to rescue him. Other people started circling. But then the school got involved. And when they got involved, it was over. Because of the eminent domain. They were going to own Athens, but they reached a deal. It was just common sense. If the school is going to build a 25 million dollar building beside you, they're going to take away your parking. And sooner or later, they're going to take you over."

After Karres made the announcement in the spring of 2016, longtime patrons were shocked, dismayed and disheartened. Yet while many landmarks in Charlotte had come down in the blink of an eye, the Double Door would not close until January 2nd of 2017, giving the venue months to stage final shows, and celebrate the venue's legacy and history. For some, it would take months for that coming finality to sink in.

"I really thought that we would see an uptick in attendance after the announcement, Nick Karres would say later. "But we really didn't. It wasn't until those last few months that people really started coming out."

One of the ways that people did respond was putting together Live At The Double Door Inn, a documentary about the history and last days of the venue. "Losing the Double Door represented a giant hole in our lives," says Jay Ahuja. "That's a big reason why I decided that a documentary needed to be made and pulled together Rick Fitts, Kim Brattain and Chuck Bludsworth as the team to do it.

"Our goal was simple. We wanted to preserve and document what the Double Door Inn had been doing for Charlotte and the entire region for the past 43 years. We were all very familiar with the place and knew we had about six months left to record the best performances and interview Nick and Matt, the longtime staffers, music promoters who worked with the club and fans."

The centerpiece of the documentary is a song by another mainstay at the Double Door, musician Randy Franklin. "We were at the club recording Jake, Rattle & Roll, a Jake Berger benefit show that featured Randy Franklin's band Crisis, among others," recalls Ahuja. "While we were setting up, Randy mentioned that he had written an original song about the club called, "I'm Gonna Miss it" and offered to let us record it. Once we heard them play it, we knew we wanted to use it, because it captures the essence of what the club meant to patrons and musicians.

"I've always thought of the Double Door as Charlotte's own Ryman Auditorium," says Randy Franklin. "As a musician it was a place that you had to earn an invitation and the privilege to play there. As a fan, I learned so much about stage presence and professionalism, as I watched my musical heroes over the years such as The Federal Bureau of Rock & Roll, The Spongetones, Cruis-O-Matic, Don Dixon, Joyous Perrin, Donna Duncan, and so many more. And the staff, they are like family to me. Playing that stage is like no other."

"Randy's song was just one of several examples of how so many people came together to help make this film better," adds Ahuja. "In addition to his song, Randy organized a CD sale and artist meet and greet to raise funds. Others donated vintage photos, video, album covers and artwork. Even the gorgeous, custom-made "Tablecaster" guitar on the cover is there because Shane Combs, who helped out with social media, connected me with Kevin Marshall at Smiling Moon Guitars.

"Hearing stories from Nick, Matt, and Mike about the early days was a treat, because the place really had a remarkable and rich musical history but it also went through some downtimes and they were able to not just survive, but thrive. Nick really had no reason to believe that this film would ever get made, but he opened up his Rolodex, sharing names and contact information readily and came to the club several times to open up in the afternoon, so we could interview folks."

"I said this in the Double Door Documentary," says producer and drummer Chris Garges, "but I really think that when a place is run by cool people, that kind of attitude and general vibe can really permeate a place. Especially if it's a place that's been there with the same cool people running it for a really long time. The Double Door is a prime example of that. It's been surrounded by wonderful people with really good intentions for a long time. I think that often times, people who run businesses can get so caught up in running them that their business interests interfere with what might have been cool about their business to begin with. I don't think that ever happened to Nick. I think he always had a genuine love of what he wanted when he started and he made decisions that helped not lose sight of that. That's rare. It sounds like some cliche fairy tale thing, but it's really true with that place."

During this time, musician Kevin Marshall got the chance to take some of the Double Door's original tables, and turn them into guitars. "My background is Tool & Die. I built high end tooling for many years. The thing that got me started was I would take an instrument to a shop for repair and when I would pick it up It was usually worse than when I took it in. I knew that if I could do Tool & Die that I could learn to be a luthier.

"I was in there one night and I told Gregg McCraw of MaxxMusic that I see a lot of guitars in this building. Gregg thought that was a great idea. He passed that on to Nick Karres. I finally got to meet with Nick and he gave me a table from the early days of the venue. It is pecan, of all woods. The pecan tables in the venue were all built by the same wood shop here in Charlotte. I wanted to stay true to the era since the Double Door was established in 1973. The hardware, the pickups and the headstock are all early 70's Fender guitar specs."

The Double Door's final weeks became a blur of the bands that had hosted so many nights at the venue. Skip Castro, Jimmy Thackery, Bob Margolin, Roomful of Blues, Tab Benoit. Some of the local musicians that had first set up in the old game room came back for final shows. Woody Mitchell, Jake Berger, Donna Duncan, Bill Noonan, and the Federal Brothers. When the Federal Bureau Of Rock & Roll reconvened for their annual show to celebrate the Double Door's anniversary, the show sold out so quickly that a second show was added. Which also sold out.

"If you think about it, we were pretty much seven days a week, almost 52 weeks a year," says Nick Karres. "We were open all the time, and even if you had a couple of people every night, that could add up to more people than any of the bigger places in town. Day in and day out, night in and night out, we brought a lot of people to Charlotte. Some nights, I knew, there's a lot of people from out of town. I'm proud of that."

"I have been playing at the Double Door since 1979 and I will always think of the dozens of gigs, hundreds of songs, and every good time I had in that club," commented Bob Margolin. "I watched friendships, romances, and endless good times there for two generations. The sound of my guitar will echo in that spot forever."

"For forty years every single group I've been involved with has played at The Double Door Inn," says Jimmy Thackery. "It has been the longest running gig I've had in all that time and the countless musical moments we have all experienced on that stage will never be replaced or forgotten. Though the cast of characters have changed many times through the decades, there was always a feeling of stability that Nick and the staff provided. Just knowing it was there was comforting somehow. Thank you Nick. Save me a brick! My last note on that stage was as filled with joy as the first one, forty years ago!"

"I've been playing the Double Door Inn since 1979, which is basically when I started my life as a touring musician," added Tinsley Ellis. "Nick has stuck with me through every band change- Alley Cats, Heartfixers, Tinsley Ellis- and through every band personnel change. Never once did he criticize the "new band guy" or compare him to the previous one. He knew it would work itself out over time. And it always does when you're in it for the long haul.

"Nick's been like a big brother to me when I needed advice, whether it be personal or professional in nature. His staff has been like siblings to me. And you know how siblings can be! I'll really miss the Double Door and the Double Door family. I wish someone would put the building on a flatbed truck, drive it slowly through the city streets in the middle of the night, and plop it down somewhere. "

On December 31st, the Spongetones returned for their last New Year's Eve show, and their last at the venue. "If the Double Door had to close, I was right where I wanted to be, on that stage with The Spongetones," says Pat Walters. "Packing up was hard. Yes, there were hard moments. Pretty much every step I took around the place, the stairs, break room, stage, even the parking lot. Knowing that it would all soon be gone was difficult. Forty years of memories of the Double Door. The music and many friends I made there did kind of play in my head."

"I had to separate myself from my emotions to do that show," says Jamie Hoover. "I wasn't going to cry, I wasn't going to do anything but enjoy it.

"I believe that it was our home base, and that we owned it. It was where my musical life began. I joined the Spongetones and married my wife in the same year. The Double Door is where I became a man."

"It was joyful and sad," says Steve Stoeckel about that night. "I was honored to be there. I loved it when we had the audience sing 'Always Look On The Bright Side Of Life', and 'In My Life.'"

As to what made the Double Door so special, Stoeckel adds, "That stage. People in your face. The sound of the room. The crowd giving back. We felt loved. We grew up there. It was Home. It was like putting on an old, comfortable pair of shoes, and then kicking down the doors for three hours with those shoes."

When you entered the Double Door Inn, the first thing you would see is the venue's poster walls, advertising upcoming shows. Slowly, the wall began to have open spaces, until it finally had one poster left. Twenty-five years previous, soundman Les Moore had put together the Monday Night Allstars as a way for some of Charlotte's best musicians to get together and play. And on January 2nd, the Allstars took to the stage for the Double Door's last show.

Throughout the night, patrons sat and talked. In the game room, on the back deck. Others stood in front of the stage, or stood near the soundboard. The bar was a busy place to be, no matter which side of the bar you were on. As the second set flowed into the third, very few went home early on this night. Lenny Federal and Wendell Elliott joined the band, as did original Allstar saxpohonist John Alexander. Nick Karres, his wife Betty, and his brother Matt also talked to many people. Hugs and thank you's were exchanged, in abundance. As the band began to play their final set, the rain began to down-pour even harder. Water began to leak through the old skylights of the venue, dripping on a few patrons. The sky is crying, Stevie Ray Vaughan once sang. But the party, and the music continued on.

As the Allstars' final set drew to a close, the band called for the audience to stand, and let go. The last song they played on this night was not a mournful one, but instead the rousing call to arms of Sly & The Family Stone's "I Want To Take You Higher". Audience member jumped together as the song's chorus was played at full volume. "I wanna take you HIGHER!!!" sang the entire room. At the end of the song, many throughout the building hugged, cried, and cheered for the night of music, and all of the music that the venue had been home to. Many that night stayed until last call, or even until they turned the lights out. It was truly a night that they did not want to see end.

The next day, Nick Karres and the Double Door staff began the process of dismantling the stage, and preparing the building to be cleared out by the end of the month. "I can't believe that we did that," Nick would say later. "There was really hard. But we had to. And if we had waited, it would have been even harder to do so."

Everything that could have been taken out of the building was, with several auctions and sales held over the next few weeks ago. Walking into the building without the stage, and all of the things that it had once held, was difficult for some. "The spirits have left the room," said one that was there. Despite the efforts of several local businessmen and citizens to get the building moved, CPCC would not allow that to happen. The physical story of the Double Door Inn would end on January 31st, when Nick Karres left the building for the last time, knowing that the building would not be there in a few short weeks.

"When you were doing it, you don't think about it," says Nick Karres. "Did I think that we were creating history? No. Now looking back, I realize that it was kind of a monumental task."

Thankfully, the music that the Double Door had been home to soon found new live in other venues. The Tuesday Night Jazz Night soon found a home at one venue, while the Monday Night Allstars took refuge in another. As did the Charlotte Blues Society. And more venues in Charlotte would soon have something that had ties to the Double Door. A soundboard, speakers, soundmen, bartenders, doormen. What once was at 218 Independence Boulevard, is now spread throughout the city of Charlotte, North Carolina, and many other places.

"The Double Door stayed true to the feel that I got from it the first time I went there," adds Pat Walters. "Unpretentious, not too big but big enough. The consistency of Nick Karres at the helm for all those years, along with many Double Door crew who spent a large piece of their lives there. The Double Door was a home for so many musicians and music lovers, and is a place that lives on in our hearts and souls."

Music is a voice. Of the people that created it, who sing it, and the places that it inhabits. For over 43 years, the Double Door Inn gave life to the music that came from within its walls. And by doing that, gave new voice to the ideas of many that enjoyed the music, enjoyed life, and wanted to take those ideas further. For those that loved it, the Double Door was more than an old house. It was a place of gathering, a solace from the madness of the everyday world, and a beautiful dream that can never be fully described, or accurately explained. The Double Door Inn passed through many of us, just as much as we passed through it. They, and we are all forever changed by the experience of the Double Door Inn, and its beautiful dream. Dirty floor, and all.

"When my brother Matt and I started the Double Door," says Nick Karres, "We

THE MONDAY NIGHT ALLSTARS, JANUARY 2, 2017.
Photos by Daniel Coston

WENDELL ELLIOTT, JANUARY 2, 2017.
Photo by Daniel Coston

wanted to provide a place for young people to go. We didn't realize that the live music thing was going to happen, but when we did, we committed ourselves to bringing the best music we could to Charlotte. There were many styles of music- reggae, zydeco, and others- that were introduced to people at our club. We committed ourselves to doing that for as long as we could.

"Thank you to all of the people over the years that supported us. Thank you to all of the entertainers and customers over the years that have now passed on, and thank you to all of the entertainers that have come in and graced our stage, and played hard. They gave great shows. and they gave it their all."

Much like the music that it gave a home to, the Double Door Inn lives on. In those that created it, played there, worked there, and passed thought it. It lives on in their memories, their hearts and minds, and those that carry its story. Like the next great song, waiting to be sung, it is out there. An unbroken circle of life, music and experience, where the "Live Blues" sign still lights up the open sky, the music plays at full volume, and the Door is always open.

THE DOUBLE DOOR INN, 1974.
Courtesy Double Door Inn archives.

www.ingramcontent.com/pod-product-compliance
Lightning Source LLC
Chambersburg PA
CBHW070925160426

43193CB00011B/1581